Healing Parties

Gail Mosley Conner, Esquire

PRESS

Healing Parties
by Gail Mosley Conner, Esquire

Printed in the United States of America

ISBN 978-1-60791-589-8

NOTE: This is not a fictional work. However, the writings only reflect fragmented memories and as such, do not represent perfection or a life story.

www.GailMConner.com

www.xulonpress.com

TABLE OF CONTENTS

ACKNOWLEDGEMENTS

I would like to acknowledge my family for all their support through the years. With special thanks and gratitude to my parents, Juanita and Otis, who gave their best and worked tirelessly to provide for our family.

I thank my husband, Curtis, *(my high school sweetheart)* for his love and support for so many years. My children, Courtney, Brian and Daniel for making being a mom so easy and enjoyable, especially the teenage years when I was able to fill my childhood voids by entertaining them and their friends at the annual Valentine's Balls that helped to heal my wounds.

I also would like to express appreciation to my in-laws, Willie James and Salomia, who have treated me as a daughter.

Congratulations to my parents, Juanita and Otis and in-laws, Salomia and Willie who have been married over 50 years.

I would like to thank the home churches in Alabama that provided the spiritual foundation for my husband and me when we were young. Without such a foundation, we would have perished.

I would like to acknowledge my Pastor, Dr. John Draper, for his teaching ministry.

I thank all of God's angels who reached out to help me along life's journey.

My most important thanks go to my Lord and Savior Jesus Christ. Thank you for choosing to save me at such a young age and being with me throughout the years. Thank you for joining me in the furnace of life and keeping the fire from destroying me.

DEDICATION

This book is dedicated to my three grandmothers. I know that some people are lucky to have two grandmothers, but I was blessed with three. All three of my grandmothers were housekeepers. I would go to work to help clean houses or offices with two of them when I was a child.

Grandma Viola

She has passed on to be with the Savior. Her love and constant support is missed. She showed me unconditional love and support. I remember and appreciate the surprise I would occasionally find in my college mail that included a note from her and $20.00 for a very broke granddaughter. I know that those little $20.00 gifts were a sacrifice for her with the very low housekeeping wages that she earned cleaning. Those $20.00s were more valuable than the purchase power that it provided to help me meet some basic needs as a college student.

Grandma Eddie Mae

She is the sister of Grandma Viola (*the Mosley girls*). She always demonstrated unconditional loved and supported for me and others. She is 95 now, but still cooking and full of infinite love. I'm still trying to master her cooking skills and recipes.

Grandma Willie Mae

She has passed on. Her courage, laughter and strength help me to get up when I fall down from the pressures in life. At times, she worked up to three jobs, just to make ends meet. I spent wonderful summers in Gulfport, Mississippi experiencing the joys and pleasures in her life and watching her make praline candies, gumbo, chicken and dumplings, and corn bread that tasted like cake.

I have tried to preserve their love and their history
by documenting and saving their recipes
from the foods that I loved as a child.

I will always love my three grandmas.

Thank you!

CHAPTER 1

THE JOURNEY HOME

Counterintuitive!

If I had to use one word to describe my life, my history, and my success, that word would be counterintuitive. Counterintuitive means – *not in accordance with what would naturally be assumed or expected. It is when a result defies the traditional basic logic – it is something that is contrary to what common sense would suggest.*[1]

The Journey Home

I finally made it home on July 11, 2006 at 7:46 a.m.

I didn't plan to make this journey. I didn't know that the journey was leading me home until I looked out the window of the plane and from a distance, with my own eyes, I could see the land that I had heard about, read about, and talked about for a lifetime. The initial glimpse of the beauty of the landscape instantly erased all the negative images that had been embedded into my perception of this land and its people. A trip not intended for me. I had made no personal plans to travel to this destination. The distance was much too far and too expensive for a family vacation, and we always traveled as a family on long trips – except for this time.

This journey began as a result of my daughter, Courtney, her love for God, and her love of helping people, no matter what continent they lived on, and her desire to do God's will with her life.

Courtney had just graduated from Goucher College, *Magnum cum Laude*, with honors in Sociology and a concentration in Social Justice. She had interviewed for jobs, but her heart was elsewhere. In the summer after her junior year of college, Courtney interned at the International Justice Mission (IJM), a Christian human rights organization, headquartered in Washington, D.C. with 16 offices around the world. I even had the opportunity to spend time in the IJM office volunteering. Little did I know that this would be the doorway to my journey home.

Reflecting on the human rights work of IJM, Courtney's heart was set on continuing her relationship with IJM, and she sought out a position with them. IJM offered her a choice of two yearlong internships after her graduation from Goucher – India or Africa. After much consideration, we believed that Africa would be an easier transition. This was going to be a huge transition for her and for us as a family. Our only daughter would be on another continent. Where would she live? What if she became ill? We couldn't be in Africa in four hours. This was also something very new for her dad and me.

When my husband and I finished college, we immediately looked for jobs. Her dad wanted her to go right to graduate school, but I wanted her to follow her heart and dare to take on life's adventures. In the black community, it is rare to finish college and take a year off volunteering, and on top of that, in a foreign country. We are not traditionally exposed to these types of experiences. My going to college in Wisconsin was considered a foreign land to my family. Our family tended to stay close to home in Alabama and Mississippi.

But, we want to support our children in pushing the limits of their capabilities and explore what this world has to offer, so they can experience what prior generations in our family lacked knowledge of or resources to pursue. I believe in pursuing what you are passionate about and taking risks and leaps of faith. What do I have to lose – *the potential of success, the chance of an adventure*? I may fail, but even with failure I gain knowledge and develop relationships from the experience.

I have learned that success in life has nothing to do with winning or losing, failing or succeeding. Rather, success in life for me has been experiencing and enjoying the journey of life. I have mastered living a successful life by learning how to take life's lemons (the sour experiences) and turning those lemons into lemonade (identifying God's blessings that add sweetness to the bitter experience that keeps you from being broken by life's circumstances, and avoiding becoming as bitter as the lemon).

Let me take you on a portion of my life's journey of lemons and hopefully you will be able to taste the lemonade (God's sweet blessings) in my life.

By the way, lemons have nutritional value and are beneficial. In the same way, the lemons in my life had value. Most of the time, I just didn't recognize the value at the time, because the bitterness of the moment made it difficult for me to recognize the benefits. But, over time, as I reflect back on my life's journey, the benefits of the lemons in my life are recognizable to me and I can see the benefits of those experiences – even the unpleasant experiences – more clearly. Now, I look forward to the lives of my children and their generation.

I am sure that my parents' generation sees even more benefits than my generation.

Something that began as a trip to support my child's passion for service in social justice resulted in a healing trip home for me.

The irony is that I didn't even know that I was homesick – until I got home.
I didn't even know that I was in need of healing.

As I continued to look out the window, the beauty of the land began to take my breath away. As a person who grew up on a farm, working the fields, harvesting crops, and tending the animals, I had developed a great appreciation for the land, plants and animals. With a love of the land and animals that runs deep within my soul. I realized that my trip to Africa was not an accident, but part of God's plan for my life, to help my wounds heal, and to allow him to show me how to further build the road to reconciliation.

As the plane continued to descend, my mind began to take me back to my childhood. I began to have fragmented memories of the past that apparently I had suppressed and buried, to be forgotten. Here I was, this black mother traveling with her now young adult daughter about to set foot on a land that she had been told for many years was the motherland, a place portrayed to us as children as something bad.

As a child, I never even thought of traveling beyond Mississippi where my maternal grandmother lived, and now I was about to set foot on the continent of my forefathers and the place where it is believed life began. This was a long way for this rural southern Alabama woman who, during the height of desegregation, was told to go back to Africa by the white folks in my community who didn't want their children going to school with me. For my generation, those who were caught up in the Civil Rights Movement after the enforcement of the court ruling in Brown v. Board of Education, we encountered experiences that encompassed two worlds. We were torn from a segregated world and thrown into a desegregated world that rejected our presence and our right to existence.

Because of those past experiences, this special trip home would culminate my life journey. It would give me what I didn't know I was searching for. It would heal my wounds and remove the scars. I had done everything that I could do in my short life. I had given it my best, no matter the circumstances, so God had a gift for me. It was an incredibly, beautiful gift that was just for me.

As I got off the plane, after a three-day journey with my daughter, I began to have this incredible feeling of joy. My heart began to race. My body began to feel different. I felt as though there was a light shining from within me. The feeling of excitement engulfed me. It was the feeling of someone riding on a white horse to come and save me from all my hurt and pain and all the bad people who had caused harm to my community and me. But, this white horse wasn't a man. It was the gift of the Father, the Son and the Holy Spirit. They came on the trip, too.

It was winter there, the weather was pleasant and the sky was clear and beautiful. As I looked around, all I saw were people who looked liked me. It was an incredible feeling – unexplainable. It was a strange feeling not being the minority. As I walked through the airport to retrieve my luggage, everyone was friendly, smiling and extremely kind. As the lady checked my passport, she looked at me and then looked at my passport again and then she said, "Are you Oprah's friend, Gail"? I smiled and said, "No, I am not that lucky in life."

My daughter and I exited the Lusaka, Zambian airport and other American interns met us to take us to the hotel.

I checked into the hotel and entered the elevator. An African gentleman who worked at the hotel helped me with my bags. He said – "Are you from America"? I answered, "Yes." Then, he said, "Is this your first time coming to Africa?" I answered, "Yes, my first trip." Then, he looked at me with a big smile and said, "Welcome home!"

The extreme kindness of the people was wonderful. The men were such gentlemen, opening the door for me and complimenting me on my beauty. Beauty. I had never been called beautiful before. The women were such ladies, kind and very soft-spoken, and extremely polite.

I needed to go to the bank. I was told that the bank was within walking distance from the hotel. I walked into the bank and saw all these people of color. I asked whom I would need to see to make a business transaction. I was directed to the desk where an African woman was seated. I asked if I could see someone who could help me with my transaction and she answered, "I can help you, I am in charge here." Then, she commented, "You must be American." I answered that I was, and then she completed the transaction, and told me to relax and enjoy my visit home. Wow, that was the second time I had been welcomed home.

She was very interested in what my life was like in America, and we talked for a while before I returned to the hotel. It was amazing. It seemed that this African woman had the same misconception of what an African-American was like as I had the wrong misconception about what a native African was like. We had a wonderful mutually beneficial exchange.

I wanted to see sights in this beautiful country, so I scheduled as many excursions as possible to the different sites in the area. I was surprised to discover that every taxi that I entered had Christian music playing and the drivers always started a conversation about God. I don't recall ever getting in a taxi in the United States and hearing any Christian music or the driver sharing his love for Jesus. That was very different, indeed.

I wanted to travel to another part of the country, so I could see as much of this land as possible during my visit. I hired a private driver, so we could travel to multiple places without a set schedule, to allow for maximum flexibility in seeing sites as we traveled. We had a female driver who was also a Christian. She was very friendly and took us to meet her family at their home in Lusaka. My daughter and two of the other interns traveled with us on this day, because we were going to Victoria Falls. I was overwhelmed at the sites and the beauty of the land.

As we traveled the countryside, we saw this giant lizard crossing the road, asbestos mines, coal just lying on the ground for the locals to pick up and use as a heating source for cooking, and pieces of stones that we discovered were used to make local handmade jewelry. The wild animals were beautiful. The zebra is my favorite animal because for me it represents perfect harmony between the two races of peoples that have impacted my life dramatically – **black** and **white** – creating beauty that only those two colors combined can ever create.

As we arrived at our final destination, Victoria Falls, the site was absolutely breathtaking. This was one of the Seven Wonders of the World that I had shared with friends' years before as being one of my favorite places that I had dreamed of visiting. I had been to Niagara Falls in New York and Canada some years earlier, but Victoria Falls was not as commercialized having only little man-made structures. The vision of the natural beauty of Victoria Falls will stay vividly in my mind, hopefully for a lifetime. I looked upon the beauty and I saw the environment as God had created it – and it was awesome! Boy can God cook! There were rainbows everywhere. The mist of the water from the falls tasted sweet. The zebras and monkeys were especially interesting to see, as I chased a monkey to try to get photos. The monkey seemed to play along with me.

As we journeyed back from Victoria Falls to Lusaka, Zambia, darkness approached. The driver played this one Christian tape the entire trip, which was beginning to drive my daughter crazy. The driver had fallen asleep at the wheel several times, so I had to stay awake and constantly talk to her to keep her alert. I offered to help drive, but she refused the offer. We pulled to the side of the road to look up at the stars. It was amazing to see the stars in a part of the world, which is located in both the southern and eastern hemispheres, south of the equator. The sky was like a very rich deep blue and the stars plentiful. There were so many stars; it looked as though the sky had the measles. It was amazing to see.

At that moment, I knew that God loved me so much that he wanted me to see his beauty on the soil of my ancestors that I never dreamed to see. He knew that my life experiences and connection to his beautiful earth would be a special experience for me since the beauty of the earth had been my survival mechanism for my entire life. First as a child subjected to rejection and ridicule by white classmates, and then later becoming a professional – after all what else could I ever consider doing other than environmental? It was as natural as breathing for me. Some people have the gift of singing or painting, but I have the gift of being connected to the beauty of the environment. I have done more than take time to smell the roses. I have watched the flowers grow! I appreciate these gifts that he has given to me, while some people may not even notice the flowers or may take them for granted.

I learned something else at that moment in time. I was already home, in the United States, before I made the journey to Africa because God is omnipotent and his presence is with me no matter where I live or where I go. I am at home wherever I lay my head, whether in Alabama, Wisconsin, Pennsylvania, or any other place that life may take me, as long as my God is with me. I was free and loved and healed in an instant. All the hurt, pain and suffering left my mind, body and soul. I didn't hurt anymore. My scars were healed. My wounds were healed. I didn't need to accomplish anything else in life. Life was complete for me, even if I didn't make it back home to the United States, because I would have lived a full life with no regrets.

I guess you are saying – what in the world does this have to do with your trip to Africa?

My trip to Africa in 2006 was the end of the journey, not the beginning.

Well, because my journey actually began around 1968.

CHAPTER 2

THE YEAR OF JOY

Fragmented memories…

It was the year 1968.
In 1968, I was supposed to be entering the fourth grade at a segregated school, attended by all blacks in my small rural Alabama farming town. This was going to be my best year in school. I would get to attend class with the students with whom I started in the first grade. What a wonderful school year. My parents were very proud of me. I was happy and I did very well. It was the best year ever! The summer was also wonderful – even as I helped to gather crops in the fields and helped with the pigs. In fact, everything was grand – I had a wonderful year. Everything was perfect. I had a pet pig, a pet cow (that my Uncle Preston had given to me as a gift), a pet dog, and a pet cat. Who could ask for anything more? God blessed me with the most wonderful year of my young life.

I enjoyed every moment, and can still recall looking for four leaf clovers in the front yard just for fun and making mud pies. I was in heaven.

Everything seemed perfect – in my little world.

I walked to my segregated school along the ditch and through the fields or by taking other short cuts. There were no sidewalks or traffic lights in my little town. A few paved roads, but mostly dirt roads – definitely no sidewalks. I walked to my Negroes-only school with my dog by my side some days. My dog, Patty, a collie mixed breed, protected me from stepping on snakes as I walked along the ditch of the highway and through the fields or paths through the people's yards in the neighborhood.

I look back at my very humble beginnings and thought my concerns at that time were reading, writing and arithmetic. Our lives were simple. We were poor, but didn't know it, as we didn't know that there was another world out there, because we were limited in so many ways. We had a Union 76 gas station where we repaired cars and pumped gas. I went to work with my parents at the service station that they owned. I was allowed to wash the windows of the cars and filled up the cars with gas. I checked the oil in the cars, the air pressure of the tires, patched tire tubes, and hung out under the cars with my dad while he made repairs. I would hand him the tools and play while he worked. I loved to use the machine that caused the car to rise up in the air. Self-service gas stations did not exist in my area during that era. Everyone expected full service when they came to the gas station. Our gas station sold bread, chips, cookies, candy, pig feet, large pickles, and bottled drinks in the soda machine (my favorite was the chocolate soda pop).

In addition to owning the small gas station, we were also farmers. When the school year ended and summer approached, it was time to harvest crops, so working in the fields was part of life for us farmers. We would pick beans, peas and okra (which would make your body itch like crazy). We would dig up the root plants like sweet potatoes. We had corn and watermelons, but I never harvested those items – my dad, uncles and other folks did that. Harvesting food was not a pleasant task.

We would get up very early in the morning when the sun was beginning to rise, so we could finish picking as many vegetables as possible before noon, because it is very hot in southern Alabama when the sun is shining above around the noon hour. We wore long sleeves and long pants to protect us from the burning sun and the bite of the mosquitoes. But, it made us very hot. I didn't know anything about sunscreen in those days.

The worst part of working in the fields was that singing sound that the mosquitoes made in your ear. It would drive me crazy. Also, I was always worried that I would see a snake in the fields. Snakes were very common in that area. But, we would compete with other folks working in the field to see who could harvest the most crops. The goal was to try to harvest 100 pounds of vegetables and to fill up several sacks or baskets with fresh vegetables. The going rate for all our hard work was about 4¢ per pound. I don't recall ever reaching that 100-pound goal.

Sometimes, I would go to the farmers' market with my dad where he would sell the crops that he had planted and harvested. It was not a lot of fun and the days would seem to go on forever, as we waited for a potential customer to purchase our products. If we had crops left over, we would just shell the beans and peas and freeze them for food to use during the winter months or return to the market to try to sell the products again the next day after the morning harvest was complete.

So, I was either at school, working or playing. But, I enjoyed my life including the farming.

My segregated elementary school was a little building with about six small classrooms, where you went from room to room along the open porch, which was attached to the front of the little building. When it rained, we would get wet going to the "all purpose room" that served as the cafeteria, the stage for plays, and other special events. The first grade class was in the room on the end of the building and the fifth grade class was on the opposite end of the building. You started first grade on one end of the building and progressed to the other end, as you grew older.

It was a wonderful place, where learning took place in an environment of love, community and strong discipline. You knew that if you disobeyed, the teacher or the principal would punish you promptly by hitting you with a ruler for minor offenses (in the hand or on the leg). Or they would use the more severe rubber discipline device (made from a piece of a worn-out car tire) that I had only heard about, that the principal had in her office. That was for the really bad children and I had no intentions of ever doing anything that would cause me to have to make a visit to the principal's office.

There were no major discipline problems that I can remember that caused classroom disruption. We didn't have "time-outs" in my generation – at least not in my world. Also, the teachers openly expressed their belief in God and my third grade teacher was also my Sunday school teacher. Thus, it was not surprising that one of her class assignments was for the class to memorize the 23rd Psalm (King James Version) in the Bible.

Psalm 23

A Psalm of David.

[1]The LORD is my shepherd; I shall not want.

[2]He maketh me to lie down in green pastures: he leadeth me beside the still waters.

[3]He restoreth my soul: he leadeth me in the paths of righteousness for his name's sake.

[4]Yea, though I walk through the valley of the shadow of death, I will fear no evil: for thou art with me; thy rod and thy staff they comfort me.

⁵Thou preparest a table before me in the presence of mine enemies: thou anointest my head with oil; my cup runneth over.

⁶Surely goodness and mercy shall follow me all the days of my life: and I will dwell in the house of the LORD forever.

In fact, she gave me a gift. The reason I know the 23rd Psalm today is because of having to memorize it in my third grade class. This is also the teacher that spanked me with the ruler because I told time the way my mom had taught me and she demanded that I do it differently. I changed the way I told time after a swat with the ruler. This is also the teacher who began correcting the way that I spoke. What is known as Ebonics today was not tolerated in her classroom. She swiftly corrected my incorrect pronunciation of the word "sammach" and told me to say it properly "sandwich" and to also enunciate the vowels and consonants correctly. The one thing that I knew during those years was that I was loved by the teachers, because they demanded excellence, and failure was not an option.

But, discipline by a non-parent was also typical during my era. Anyone could and would discipline you no matter where you were. If an adult observed you doing something inappropriate, they would approach you and verify your family identity by saying something like, "Aren't you Buck and Juanita's child?" They would say something like, "You know that your parents wouldn't want you to do that" or "You know better than to behave like that – I am gonna tell your mamma and daddy what you did and you are going to git it when you git home."

But, it didn't end with the reprimand of someone in the community, at church or at school. The worst part was that by the time you got home (during the era of no cell phones, no home computers, no Internet, and no pagers), your parents already knew that you had gotten reprimanded. So, you had the potential of getting disciplined again when you arrived home, because your conduct required the actions of someone in the community, church or school.

There was a zero tolerance for inappropriate child behavior in the community, church or school where I grew up. They would even reprimand you for your posture and appearance by saying things like, "Stand up straight, girl" or "Act like a lady and cross your legs properly" or "Where is your hat, little girl? You know that it is too hot to be outside in this heat without a hat." Everyone showed responsibility in managing the conduct of the children – which resulted in my being a product of a Village of Disciplinary Support!

Of course, everyone was not nice with his or her comments. Sometimes the comments would be hurtful. Overall, I am grateful for every step taken on my behalf by others, because in my era, a wrong step in a segregated society could result in death to you and potential destruction of your family. There were boundaries that we had to live within, and the village approach protected all of us from harm. It taught me to cope with whatever circumstances I had to deal with in life. I learned to take obstacles that may destroy me and developed new skills and abilities to overcome and sometimes excel under the challenge. It is indeed a unique gift that is only acquired as a result of enduring the refiner's fire in the furnace of life.

I loved school, I loved learning. It was always joyful for me in the classroom. During the beginning of my fourth grade school year, I was told that I was going to be moved into Mr. Alexander's class. But, Mr. Alexander's class is the fifth grade class. Wow – that is wonderful! I got to go to class with the fifth graders instead of with the fourth graders! This was especially important to me, because I had started the first grade with those students years before, but was removed from the first grade after another parent in the community objected because her son had been born only a few days after I had been born. She insisted on her son attending the first grade early if I was allowed to attend early. Both of our birthdays fell after the cut-off date (November) for admission to school in September.

We would both have to wait a year to start first grade, unless an exception was made for our early attendance. No exception was made, so I was removed from the first grade. My heart was broken. I was learning so much and I was doing as well as the other students. There was no kindergarten, so the only pre-school preparation I had received was from my parents and a lady who attended the local church that had a brief summer program that ended each day with a Bible story and treat for the children. So, this unexpected move into Mr. Alexander's fifth grade class put me where I knew I belonged.

This was indeed The Year of Joy!

CHAPTER 3

DESEGREGATION — HELL ON EARTH

Fragmented memories…

It was the year 1969. This was the point in time that changed everything for me. The point in time where I was swept up into the storms of life created by others, that I didn't fully understand. Those days of long walks home from my Negroes-only school in the hot heat had come to an end and a new era for my generation had emerged. I had no control over the changes being forced upon me. My eyes would soon be opened, as we desegregated schools and got a peek into the lives of "white folks" – the other world.

There was another world that I didn't know about. I didn't really know anything about segregation. My parents didn't talk about those types of things. We just lived quietly in the community going to church on Sundays, tried to make a living by working hard through raising crops for harvest, working at the gas station pumping gas, and fixing cars. I didn't know anything about Jim Crow laws, court decisions (Plessy v. Ferguson or Brown v. Board of Education), the right to vote, civil rights, or anything like that. I also did not know about another case that was impacting my life – the Mobile County public school *Birdie Mae Davis* desegregation case that was filed on March 27, 1963. This was a major case that was filed to pursue the goal of desegregation of the public school in Mobile County, Alabama.[2] This case directly impacted my life.

These were cases that I was too young to know about or understand the consequences of the actions taken by others. The Birdie Mae Davis case started before I attended elementary school and would continue after I graduated from a desegregated high school. This case continued for decades, from March 27, 1963 until the 1990s. On top of all the judicial decisions, Dr. Martin Luther King, Jr. was shot and killed – assassinated at 6:01 p.m. on April 4, 1968, the year before I was sent to a desegregated school in Alabama! All of these things changed my life forever. The summer of 1969 marked an end of an era for me and the dawn of a new day. I was caught in the middle of the crossfires of change, headed for the front lines on the battlefield, as an elementary school student. I was thrown into a battle that would continue for decades. I wondered if I was properly armed for the battle that I would be required to fight.

Dad's Talk about Change

Toward the end of the summer, things seemed to be different at home. My parents seemed worried and stressed. My dad was not much of a talker. In fact, I would consider him very quiet. So, when my dad called me into the kitchen to have a talk with me that was troubling, to say the least. My two sisters were not in the room with me that day. My older sister, Sandra, was a high school student and probably knew what was about to happen to the schools, and my younger sister, Darlene, was just a baby. I began to get nervous and my body was filled with anxiety. What was wrong? Why does everyone seem worried? Why is everyone sad and afraid? What is an assassination? Why is everyone upset? What are you talking about — Martin Luther King? Please help me! What is going on? Who was murdered? What does all of this have to do with me? What have I done? Is there anything I can do to make things go back to the way they were? Somebody, please help me! I am having a mental meltdown. Can somebody tell me what is going on?

Well, I lived to regret those words. I wish that I had thought about my mom's policy of keeping your mouth shut. But, the words that came out of his mouth changed my life forever. He said, "Gail, things are changing. You are going to have opportunities that your mother and I never had. You have to remember that you are very smart and you can do anything that you put your mind to. Now you are going to have a chance to be anything that you want to be." My dad said that I was even smart enough to become a doctor someday or anything else that I could dream of becoming. But, I had to get an education, in order to have any possibility of making those dreams become a reality. Dad continued, "There is nothing more important than getting an education. So, you are to go to school and go to college, because you have the ability to do it, you have the potential to succeed!" I stood there not understanding the message that he was delivering until he said the worst words and the best words of my life, "This year, you will be going to school with white children."

Oh, my Lord! Nothing that he could have said could have prepared me for what was about to come. But, somehow, his words did matter, because they became embedded in my foundation. *I can do anything* was one of the few things that I had to hold onto for the years to come.

My dad never talked about race or the disadvantages of being black, or female, or anything like that. He taught me to do the same things that he had learned to do, regardless of my gender. It didn't matter whether we worked on a car or installed sheetrock in a house. He always showed me how to do everything that he knew how to do. He would even ask me to read the blueprints of buildings and do the calculations. I was young, female and black, but it didn't matter. He was always sharing his knowledge with me. Even though he didn't have a college degree, he was definitely a "jack of many trades."

Dad gave me that little talk, and I never responded or asked a question. I just said, "Yes, sir" when he had finished speaking. I went back to playing outside and enjoying the remainder of the summer. But, August soon approached and things seemed the same until as the days grew closer to the beginning of the school year, I noticed that the anxiety level in the home, in the community, and at church seemed very different. It felt the same as when someone close to you dies and, after the funeral, there is the feeling of discomfort inside that can't be put into words. That's how it felt at that moment in time.

Torn from One World and Thrown into Another World – Headed for the Promised Land by Force

The safe, happy life that I knew and loved had come to an end.

Things changed forever and the quiet sounds of the birds singing, the dog barking, and the pigs squealing was all drowned out by the new sound, beginning the first day of attending a desegregated school.

Dad's talk in no way prepared me for what I was about to face as an elementary school student in southern Alabama — *Dixieland*. The first thing that happened was that they split up my community and divided us among three different schools. So, the first casualty of desegregation was that my best friend, who only lived a few miles away, was sent to another school system. I soon found out that I would be on this journey alone – without my best friend.

But, wait, things got worse. I was sent to a school that landed me in the heart of the Ku Klux

Klan (KKK) territory – W.C. Griggs Elementary in Tillman's Corner — an all-white community. White students were supposed to come to my Negroes-only school, but the conditions were determined to be too inferior for white students to attend. Thus, the Negroes-only elementary school that I had attended for the previous four years was immediately closed.

Desegregation resulted in my being bused to an all-white school. That was fine with me, because I would rather take my chances on the bus any day, instead of walking in the ditches along the road, taking short cuts though fields, trying to avoid snakes. But, I would miss picking wild blackberries along the way, feeling the sunshine on my face, and the safety and love in my classroom by teachers that cared not only about me, but my success.

The life that I knew that was created by Plessy v. Ferguson, 163 U.S. 537 (1896),[3] was terminated by Brown v. Board of Education of Topeka, 347 U.S. 483 (1954).[4] These two landmark U.S. Supreme Court cases determined my past and my future.

But, I soon found out that riding the bus would be my worst nightmare. In fact, the first day of attending the desegregated school was the worst day of my life!

The school bus came and stopped at the end of our dirt road on the adjacent paved highway. It was early morning when I was picked up and the bus was almost empty. We were told to load the bus from the back. I did as I was told. I sat down and stayed quiet and watched as we made stops along the way to pick up both Negro children and white children.

It was my first and the longest bus ride I have ever had. As we stopped, I began to notice how nice the homes were of the white children who got on the bus. No one gave eye contact. Everyone seemed afraid, at least on that first day. We finally approached the new school. There was a graveyard to my left and the school to my right. As the bus approached, I could hear yelling, screaming and cursing, "Nigger @#&. Go home, Niggers. Go back to Africa."

As I looked out of the windows of the bus, the graveyard across the street seemed a more pleasant place than the elementary school that the bus had approached. Oops – I wouldn't be welcome in the graveyard next door either because I forgot it's for whites only.

There were picket signs and all those white people yelling at us. There were a lot of people standing outside my new elementary school. It was disturbing. I was afraid. Why do they hate me so much? They don't even know me? I am a good girl.

As I got off the bus, I was afraid to look around. I stepped off the bus and followed the crowd of students as they entered the building. I finally looked up as I entered the building. My mouth flew open as I gazed upon the inside of the school. Wow, this is beautiful! It's so big. Oh my goodness, they have a library – a real library –with so many books. This looks like something that I would see on television. They have a hallway inside the building. The cafeteria is inside the building, too! I won't get wet anymore when it rains while I'm going to lunch. They have so much stuff. They have everything. This school looked nothing like the little Negro school that I had attended, my parents had attended, and my grandparents had attended in my community.

I didn't know anything about Plessy v. Ferguson and the "Separate but Equal" doctrine, but the segregated Negro school that I had attended for the previous four years was definitely not equal in quality, size or resources, or in any other way, to this all-white school that I was standing in on that day. At least that was the appearance on the surface. But, as I entered the school, I saw a lot of unfamiliar faces. I noticed that there was no eye contact from the white students. The whites were in their groups and the blacks were in their groups. We were inside a white school with white parents and white protestors outside screaming and yelling. I didn't see any black parents.

As I walked down the hall to find my classroom, I didn't see any black teachers. Oh no, how was I going to make it through this day? I am not prepared for this day. I began to pray to myself, "Lord, please have mercy on my soul. Lord, please have mercy on my soul!" With each step I prayed for mercy. My head was down, my hands were shaking, my stomach was in knots, and I couldn't breathe. I thought to myself, "Why have I been left alone to fight this battle? Why me? Why can't someone else do this instead of me? Why do I have to suffer through this?"

As I walked up to my classroom, I noticed that I was in the fifth grade (again). I thought that I would be with the sixth graders, since I was with the fifth graders last year. My heart sank and I felt defeated. Everything I had gained had been lost overnight.

This is the second time I would enter the same grade twice – first grade and now fifth grade. Every gain ultimately resulted in a loss.

Others had decided my fate, and there was nothing that I could do about it. As I looked around, I only saw white faces. I didn't recognize anyone. I was in a foreign land with foreign people who hated me just because of the color of my skin. As I was about to give up in despair, I looked at the teacher at the desk – I had been sent an Angel. God truly loved me, because the teacher at that desk was Mr. Alexander! Praise the Lord – he was an answer to my prayer. I felt like the three Hebrew boys in the Bible that were thrown into the blazing furnace (Shadrach, Meshach and Abednego).[5] King Nebuchadenezzar threw them into the furnace, and the Lord joined them in the fire. I was indeed thrown into the blazing furnace of desegregation on that day in 1969. And, the Lord joined me by sending me the only familiar face that could help me through what was about to happen to me, Mr. Alexander, the same teacher that I had had in the segregated Negroes-only school the previous year.

They had split the Negro students, and as a result, we were scattered among the different classes – mostly isolated and alone. The Negro children from my community were scattered among schools and then scattered again within the classrooms in the schools.

Later that day, the class was sent outside for playtime. I thought that maybe I could make some friends, and then, everything would be fine. Surely, if I am very nice to the white girls, they will let me play with them. I had picked up a basketball and started bouncing it on the playground. I noticed that a group of white girls were looking at me. One of the girls started walking toward me and my heart filled with joy – *they are going to play with me and then everything will be fine*. The blonde little girl came toward me. She looked at me. I smiled and began to get excited thinking, "Wow, I think that she is going to ask me to play with her." But, the words that came from the mouth of the girl crushed my hopes instantly, as she yelled to me, "Hey, Nigger, give me that ball!" I didn't respond to her, because I was not a Nigger, and I kept the ball and played alone.

I don't think that I could ever forget her name, even though I have tried. I would later come in contact with her again on the Varsity Cheerleading Team at the local high school that I attended. She was also on the prestigious Azalea Trail Maid court with me, which was the highest honor for select Southern girls born in Mobile, Alabama.

God gave me Mr. Alexander to help me cope during the first year of desegregation. Mr. Alexander would play the tic tac toe game with me sometimes, because I hated to go outside and watch the girls and boys play and exclude me. I was comforted by his presence and I felt protected from my surroundings. He provided me with a safe haven during the first year of desegregation. He seemed to need me as much as I needed him, because the joy and laughter that I had experienced the year before from this same teacher in the Negroes-only elementary school was not the teacher that was present in this new white school. It seemed that we were both alone and hurting.

CASUALTIES OF DESEGREGATION

I was beginning to adjust to all the changes in my life. The anxiety that I felt did not end when I got off the school bus and arrived home. My parents had no idea what I was going through. But, desegregation caused other heartache for our family. After the schools were desegregated, other sectors began to desegregate. All of a sudden, Negroes could go through the front door of the white-owned restaurants and other establishments, instead of the back door, to place and pick up an order. This wave of access impacted our small business, the Union 76 gas station. Negroes could now buy gas from the white companies. This resulted in our family's small business customer base vanishing. We continued to operate, but eventually, the business would suffer its final deathblow when a hurricane destroyed the building. We couldn't afford to re-build. Unfortunately, our local Negro-owned business was another casualty of desegregation.

There were a lot of fun memories experienced there. My dad would allow customers to buy gas on credit, and also allow them to get auto repairs on credit. They didn't have credit cards.

This was the same era when George Wallace stood in front of the University of Alabama and vowed to fight to keep Negroes out of the institution. Our community and my family fought back and boycotted the local white-owned grocery store (the only grocery store in our community), because the store had a George Wallace sign in the window. We would have to drive to another community to purchase groceries. I didn't like the store in the other community, because it smelled horrible. But, my family refused to support the business that supported a political figure that was against desegregation.

It was the first time that I experienced first-hand the impact of consolidated community action (referred to as grassroots organizing today) taken by the powerless. It was a form of peaceful community organization. I learned at that moment in time, that no one is completely powerless. You always have a choice. You can operate from a position of fear and take whatever those in control determine is the limit for your life, your family's life, and your community. Or, you can use the power of "choice" to change the conduct of those unhealthy systems. As a result of this experience, during my early years "community organizing" was embedded into my soul, thus impacting all my life relationships and actions.

It doesn't matter how vulnerable you are. There is always a way to overcome the obstacles in your life. *As I have always said – if the door closes in your face, look for a window!* If you can't find a job, create your own job by starting a small business with the gift God has already given to you. Turn your obstacle into your stepping stone. Turn your lemon into lemonade. Never let someone else determine your destiny. No one has control over your soul except for God. Claim your victory and armor yourself with God's Word, and enter the battle to win!

No matter how bad things are in your life, there is a way out. God always provides a way out. Your time may not be his time, but you can choose to persevere, stay strong, and never give up. I am speaking from firsthand experience that I can personally testify to – not from a book that I have read or someone else's philosophy about life.

My life has had its share of struggles. I have had more than my fair share of lemons in my life. Life isn't always fair, But, I only have one life, so I make the best of each day that God blesses me with, because I will never live that day again. Sometimes, I feel as though I live a world within a world. I live in a spiritual bubble completely on faith each day for God to meet all my needs. I just try not to worry about tomorrow, because God's Word says that we should not worry about our life. All we have to do is to allow him to drive as we follow the direction that he directs us to travel. In the book of Matthew, Chapter 6, beginning at verse 25, the answer to worrying is clearly addressed as follows:

Matthew 6: 25-34

Do Not Worry
Therefore I tell you, do not worry about your life, what you will eat or drink; or about your body, what you will wear. Is not life more important than food, and the body more important than clothes? Look at the birds in the air; they do not sow or reap or store away in barns, and yet your heavenly father

feeds them. Are you not much more valuable than they? Who of you by worrying can add a single hour to his life? And, why do you worry about clothes? See how the lilies of the fields grow. They do not labor or spin. Yet I tell you that not even Solomon in all his splendor was dressed like one of these. If that is how God clothes the grass of the field, which is here today and tomorrow is thrown into the fire, will he not much more clothe you, O you of little faith? So, do not worry, saying, What shall we eat? Or what shall we drink? Or what shall we wear? For the pagans run after all these things, and your heavenly Father knows that you need them. But seek first his kingdom and his righteousness, and all these things will be given to you as well. Therefore do not worry about tomorrow, for tomorrow will worry about itself. Each day has enough trouble of its own.

Casualty – Loss of Structure and Discipline

There was another casualty of desegregation. I would later realize that the best year of my public school education life was spent in a segregated school that lacked all the wonderful resources that were available to the white children of the same age who also lived in my community. There was something more valuable than the books, buildings and educational resources that was lost to desegregation – the love, care, structure, and discipline that were present in the Negroes-only schools. The rules were firm and the discipline severe, but we learned in a controlled and managed environment that included love and the desire to educate us, so we could become productive members of society. That discipline extended into the community.

With desegregation, the familiar school discipline was lost overnight. Control and discipline were lost with the changes and lack of trust between the two races. The Negro students began to transform in this new environment with conflicts between the races at times resulting in riots. School was cancelled many times, because of racially intense riots. I no longer felt safe at school. I no longer enjoyed school. School became a place of fear and anxiety.

The community discipline also eventually vanished. Everything had changed. Families became isolated, dealing with their children's education as an individual family, instead of as a community. We were no longer the community that existed before desegregation.

Casualty – Loss of Music and Social Life

Another initial casualty of desegregation was the loss of our music and social life standards. We were desegregated into the white culture, instead of integrated into each other's cultures to create an opportunity for respect and appreciation in this new racially diverse educational system.

I was excited when it was announced at my elementary school that a "sock hop" event was being held. I didn't know what a "sock hop" was, but I was excited to attend any type of social event that would be held at my new school. I followed my classmates to the room where the "sock hop" was going to be held. They seemed happy and excited. As I entered the room, I saw children everywhere, children whom I had never seen before. It was quiet, except for the talking, giggles and occasional laughter from a group of girls standing in the corner. Then, they began to play music. What is that song? I have never heard music like that before. What are they talking about in that song, "Jeremiah Was a Bullfrog" – what kind of music was that? Well, more songs like that were played at the "sock hop" during the entire event. Where is the Motown music? I don't remember hearing even one familiar song that was played that I, as a black child, could identify with. Our music and social life at school were gone, too.

At the time, it seemed that we had to give up everything recognizable and familiar to us, just so we could go to school with children of a different race. In exchange, we would have to give up everything familiar to us – even the music and the way we interacted socially. Is such a price worth the intended reward? I just didn't understand why all of this was happening to me and where the benefits of all this change could be found. My eyes couldn't recognize any benefit – at least, not then.

At my first school dance, the "sock hop," I realized that the dance was not intended for me.

Attending school with another race was the only achievement, because initially, socially, the races grew up separately. We only interacted in school. I wasn't aware of any non-school interaction between the races. But, this first step laid the foundation for change that would alter my life, create new opportunities for my generation, and heal a nation. I didn't know it at that time, but my parents knew it, and that was the message that my dad was trying to share with me that hot summer day in 1969.

Casualty – Weakening of the Public School System

Private schools began to emerge as the new educational system in the U.S. With elite schools for the wealthy and privileged expanded the power of the legacies to gain access to the top universities and colleges in the years to come. The most fascinating thing was the emergence of white church schools throughout the south, where parents chose a potentially inferior education for their white children in these church schools over a traditional public school education with the Negroes. Both the poor whites and the Negroes were left to attend the rapidly deteriorating public educational system or the newly created church schools and other schools for those who could not afford to attend the wealthy private schools.

Instead of uniting around desegregation to protect the quality of the public educational system, the white community, including the white Christian community, chose to abandon the public school system. The irony is that the disenfranchised Negro and the whites, who could not afford the elite private schools, both suffered because of the breakdown of the public school system that was the access point to the American dream by both groups of people.

The emergence of two societies was the ultimate result. It was like a set of twins being born – one black and one white. But, they couldn't get past the color of their skin to see that, other than their color, they both were identical in almost every other way, and in need of the same thing to have access to their version of the American Dream: a good education, at that time, only available through the public school systems for people who had limited financial resources.

What an America we could have if only those who embrace the Confederate Dixie Flag would unite around a common cause with the people of different races. We do have a common cause – *we want the best for our children, and educational access is the key to them having a chance at the best!* With the way things are going globally, maybe it is time for reconciliation of all American people, including those who embrace the Confederate Flag, and time to reevaluate who is the real enemy. Your enemy is not me!

CHAPTER 4

THE SCIENCE PROJECT THAT SAVED ME

Fragmented memories…

The sixth grade, my last year in this elementary school, was even more challenging than the fifth grade. Mr. Alexander wasn't there for me anymore. In fact, I had a white female teacher who was verbal about her position against desegregation. She didn't allow her daughter to attend the school that she was assigned to because there were too many blacks at that school. So, her daughter was in my class for the school year. This teacher was hard to please. No matter what I did to try to please her, she was never satisfied. She seemed to ignore my existence and interacted with me as little as possible.

Now, being in the classroom during recreational breaks was no longer a haven of safety for me. Going outside was a break from the pressure of being in the class. So, I would go outside, but most of the time, there was no one to play with. Sometimes, some of the boys would talk to me, but, for the most part, the girls avoided interacting with me. I would just sit and try to make it through the day. Sometimes, when I felt really alone, I would lie down on my back on the grass and just repeat the 23rd Psalm, while I looked into the skies above.

Then one day, a science project was assigned that required the students to document the types of clouds in the sky each day, and then forecast the weather patterns, based upon the information collected. That project was exciting. It was my angel. I became so captivated by the weather project that I continued to track the clouds even after the assignment was over.

I had found my new friend that would be my friend for life that no one could take away from me, no matter where I was. I discovered the environment! I fell in love with everything that the environment had to offer: clouds, plants, insects, moon, stars, water, and wind/air. I could remember the sweet smell of wild honeysuckle. I enjoyed the simple pleasures of watching the butterflies and picking the wild flowers. I realized the harsh reality of my circumstances and that I could not rely on others to be my source of joy or happiness.

These challenges in my life began to create the foundation for my profession in life. A lemon was turned to lemonade for me, as a result of that science project. I would be the happiest on the playground after I found my new friends in life – God's beautiful creations – his wonderfully, beautiful environment. I discovered science!

This science project created a new focal point for me during these years of change. Instead of praying that I would find someone to be my friend in class, I connected to the natural beauty of the environment that God gave to me. At night, I would look at the stars and it would give me joy. I would spend time with my pets and other animals. I learned new survival techniques and, as a result, I no longer felt rejected by those who considered me objectionable, because of the color of my skin.

As a result of this science project, I began to focus on the things that man or woman couldn't change: the stars, the sun, the moon, and the clouds. These things were out of the control of humans (and out of the control of those little girls), and I was able to cope with the educational environment that was forced upon me. Now when the girls would pass out party invitations in class and skip my desk, it didn't bother me anymore. I would just look outside and focus on something in nature that they couldn't change and smile at God's creations. It is probably no accident that I am a biologist, environmentalist and environmental attorney. It's a natural accumulation of my past experiences, which started with this science project.

There is a song that reminds me of the feeling that I felt when I discovered the environment in elementary school. The chorus of the song is *"The world didn't give it and the world can't take it away."*

I was not aware of the existence of environmental careers when I was a child, but I became a fledgling scientist and environmentalist during the turbulent years of desegregation in the late 60s. Other events in my life would further shape my life and determine my future career.

I didn't go to school and then choose to go into a field of study. I evolved into a career that only I can do the way that I do it, because of my life experiences. There are those who are gifted to sing, dance, draw, or play a musical instrument. I received the gift of environmental science, a gift that helped me cope during a difficult phase in my life at a very young age, during the early stages of desegregation in southern Alabama – *Dixieland*.

CHAPTER 5

THE PATH LESS TRAVELED

Fragmented memories…

You Win Your Best Battles with Your Mouth Shut

I was destined to take a path less traveled. From the beginning of my childhood, I was always told that I was different. Being told that I was different caused me concern, initially because I assumed that something was wrong with me if I wasn't like everyone else. I wanted to fit in and please my parents and others in my life's circle. So, it was disturbing to be told that I was different. I looked in the mirror one day and didn't like what I saw before me. A dark skinned black girl. I couldn't sing, I was horrible at sports, I was an average dancer, and I was the constant target of bullying by other students on the school bus rides home. To make matters worse, my mom prohibited me from fighting back from any verbal or physical attacks from other students. My mom had a strict policy of behavior upon leaving the homestead, "*You win your best battles with your mouth shut*" and she followed up with a strict unwavering policy with the clear instruction that if you chose to fight back, you will get a "whipping" when you got home. The odds were not in my favor. I don't recall ever getting into fights in school, no matter what abuse was inflicted upon me.

However, as an adult, I realized that that strict social policy probably saved me from severe injury, because considering my poor athletic abilities, no siblings in school with me to help, no brothers to protect me, and my size in comparison to the bullies when I was young, I would have surely lost every fight. My mom's policy of keeping silent no matter who lashed out against me protected me and ensured that I came home with minimal (hopefully no) physical injuries.

Revival

Uncle Preston approached me one day and asked me if I knew who Jesus was and asked if I had accepted Christ into my life as my personal Savior. I told him that I had not done so. He told me that revival was about to start (as always in August at my home church in Alabama). He said that those who are unsaved should sit on the "mourning bench," so we could pay close attention to the messages being preached during the weeklong revival. I did as I was told and sat on the "mourning bench" which is the front pew closest to the pulpit. I was happy to see other children whom I knew were also on the mourning bench, so it didn't seem so bad after all. I sat and listened, as did the other children.

As I recall, the first night passed and no one moved from the mourning bench.

The second night passed and no one moved from the mourning bench.

The third night passed and no one moved from the mourning bench.

The evening before leaving for church revival on the fourth night, Uncle Preston approached me and asked me if I had been listening to the messages spoken each night, and I replied, "Yes sir." He asked if I understood what I was hearing, and I replied, "Yes sir." He asked if I had felt anything that would lead me to make a personal decision to accept Christ as my personal Savior and I replied, "Yes sir." Then he asked, "Then, why haven't you gone up and made a public acceptance all week?" I answered, "Because I was waiting on everyone else to go up, so I wouldn't be alone." Then he spoke words to me that changed my path in life forever. He said, "I thought that you were listening to the sermons each night." I answered that I had been listening. And he asked me, "Then, what has been the message all week?" I answered, "The message has been 'DON'T FOLLOW THE CROWD.'" He looked at me and asked the final question, "Then, WHY ARE YOU FOLLOWING THE CROWD?"

At that moment, my life changed forever. I listened that evening during the revival to the message brought before the congregation by a guest minister from the north (I think Michigan). I walked up alone that night and accepted Christ alone. I realized that acceptance of Christ was a personal decision and involved a personal relationship. It was not a group decision. At that moment, all of life's decisions for me were personal decisions not decisions made for me by someone else. As a result, everything about my life has been atypical, because I don't follow the crowd. Instead, I make decisions based upon my personal beliefs and convictions. However, I don't force my beliefs upon others.

I later realized that it was basically a message on avoiding peer pressure (childhood, teen, adult, business, political, and social). That sermon and message helped me cope with desegregation. Instead of seeing the glass as half empty (the white girls won't play with me or invite me to parties), I saw the glass as half full (so what if they don't play with me or invite me to parties – I don't need to be with the crowd anyway). Now, what else can I find in my surroundings to give me joy – THE ANSWER – **GOD GAVE ME THE ENVIRONMENT** – the stars, the moon, the flowers, the insects, the plants, the sun, and the **SON**! God knew that my journey in life would involve a lifetime of walking alone. So, he prepared me for the journey early in my life through the message of salvation that he had prepared just for me. I was that important to the almighty living God that he would send a preacher from the north to lead a little black girl in the south.

I longed for childhood relationships in my new world, inclusive of children from the other race, but these relationships were not critical to my survival or success. Yes, God had a plan for my survival and that plan meant my walking a path less traveled – a path that would have been very lonely, but for the gift of that special sermon, the beauty of nature that God blessed me to see as though he created it all just for me.

With childlike joy, I began my journey traveling alone after being thrown into the rivers of changing times in 1969. As a result of my past experiences, I learned early in life to do what I believe God is directing me to do, instead of looking for the approval or disapproval of other people. You see, the world didn't give me my joy, so the world can't take it away. I learned another life lesson – "God is our refuge and strength, a very present help in trouble." I am never alone, because God is always with me. King David summed it up perfectly in Psalm 139.

Psalm 139, Verses 1-4

"For the director of music. Of David.

[1] You have searched me, LORD, and you know me.
[2] You know when I sit and when I rise; you perceive my thoughts from afar.

³ You discern my going out and my lying
down; you are familiar with all my ways.
⁴ Before a word is on my tongue you,
LORD, know it completely.

The Little Boy with the Incredible Singing Voice

While in church one day, I noticed a little boy
walking toward the front of the church. He was a
stranger. He didn't attend our church. He and his dad
were special guests. I eagerly waited on the boy's
father to get up and begin singing. But, the little boy
walked up toward the front of the church and started
singing and my heart melted. Oh my goodness, what
a beautiful voice coming out of this handsome little
boy. He seemed to be about my age, I didn't know
who he was, but I hoped that one day I would meet
him again. I was sitting on the back pew in church.
He never saw me and we never spoke. But, his voice
I would never forget.

Time passed, but when I was in the eighth grade,
I went to a high school choir concert with my cousin.
I was in middle school. I was wearing a new orange
plaid dress-pantsuit that had been made by my great-
aunt (Grandma Viola's sister - one of the Mosley
girls). I was sitting in the room and this boy walked
in. My cousin introduced me to him and said that his
name was Curtis. When he spoke to me, my heart
melted, because that was the boy. That was the same
boy who sang at my church that day years before!
I would know that voice anywhere – that beautiful
voice that melted my heart. He was very polite, such

a gentleman, and still very handsome. Oh no, he was definitely out of my league. He would never be interested in a farm girl like me. We never saw each other or spoke in any way after that brief encounter that day, until …

I started high school the next year and entered the ninth grade. As I was walking down a school hallway one day, I looked around my locker and noticed this young boy with a very neat Afro hairstyle, wearing stack shoes and bell-bottom pants looking in my direction. Oh my, it's that handsome boy with the wonderful voice again.

I was getting my books for my next class out of my locker. I turned around and there was Curtis standing by me at my locker. Then he said hello. My heart melted as he spoke to me. I don't remember anything else that he said at that moment. But, eventually, I heard the words, "algebra class" and then I said to him, –"What did you just say to me?" Then, he said to me, "Are you taking Mr. Rudder's algebra class?" I answered, "Yes, I am in that class." He said, "Great, maybe we can compare notes, because I heard that he is a very difficult teacher." I answered, "Yes, I know. I heard the same thing, but I think that I can handle the challenge."

We weren't in the same algebra section, but we shared notes and math problem formulas and started a friendship. He was an 11th grader and dating some other very popular, attractive girl at the time, and I didn't seem like the type of girl that he would consider dating. He seemed to go for those tall, attractive, model types of girls. I didn't wear makeup, was 5'2" and possibly smelled like my dog that I petted before I got on the bus for school.

But, I decided to make a prayer request, and at that moment in ninth grade with childlike faith, I asked God for that little boy to be my husband. There was something about him that I can't explain. I am the type of person who will order the same item on a menu for 20 years and never even bother to try a new dish. Once I know what I like, I am very happy and content, unless I am given a reason to try something new. I save my experimentation in life to reconstructing recipes, resolving problems that have no apparent solution, and turning the lemons in my life into lemonade. I made major decisions in my life at a very young age, with the most important decision being my desire to accept Christ as my personal Savior. Therefore, choosing a mate at that age was no stretch for me.

I wasn't looking for it, but it happened and I made a choice. At that moment, I had decided whom I wanted to be with for the rest of my life, so I prayed a brief prayer to God...

"Give me Curtis for my husband or give me a dog and I will spend my life with animals and go to medical school." I was young but I knew what I wanted and I was not afraid to ask for it on that day.

Of course, Curtis had no idea that I had chosen him. So, I had to wait and see whether he would also choose me. That was completely out of my control and not my decision to make. God doesn't force his will upon people. Each person has a choice regarding whether to invite Jesus into his or her life. A person has a choice in choosing a soul mate. It is a personal choice for each individual to make. I had made my choice, and if Curtis decided that I was not his choice, I had opted for a dog and had decided to take a specific career direction. There was no second choice for me. He was special and I knew it from the first time that I saw him.

For me to make such a bold request was not easy. It was indeed difficult, because someone whom I loved so much had fallen in love with a man at a very young age and had a child for him during an era when out-of-wedlock pregnancies were very difficult for any young woman to handle. He and only he had this special place in her heart. She chose him, but he chose someone else. Even though the choice that she made with her heart was made before I was born, her love for him was still apparent in her old age, even though she had married someone else and never spoke of her love for that person to me or others. No one could replace that person in her life, not even a husband, and she was unable to hide her love for him. No, I had no desire to be that woman, but love has a way of taking over when you least expect it, and there is nothing that you can do about it – no matter your age. Years ago, I sensed the fear in my mother when she easily recognized that type of love that I had for Curtis. She even warned me of the potential for a tragic ending with a broken heart. But, it was too late. Someone who barely knew my name had already taken my heart.

Curtis seemed to be really impressed with my math and analytical skills in algebra, so he sometimes came to me to discuss test preparation and other class assignments. Before I knew it, we were very good friends and spent a lot of time just talking and laughing. Then, one day, he said, "Do you want to go steady?" Wow! I can't believe it. Of course I answered, "Yes!" But, I told him that my parents were very strict, so I couldn't really talk to boys on the phone and couldn't go out on dates. My parents were really into this "getting an education thing" and didn't want boys to get in the way of my future. He understood, so we kept our relationship simple with interactions mostly limited to school and school activities. We did meet at the Winter Formal High School Dance that year and the photo is currently hanging in our home. In the picture, I have on a pink dress (which is my favorite color) with ruffles that my great-aunt made for me, and he was dressed nicely and sporting an Afro.

Our Secret Date – and the Big Brown Teddy Bear

My older sister was dating Curtis' first cousin. One night, my sister wanted to go to the movies with her boyfriend. My parents told her that she could go to the movies, but she had to take me with her on the date. My sister's boyfriend arrived at our home. Her boyfriend came to the door to greet my sister prior to leaving for the evening. I got in the back seat of my sister's boyfriend's car. We drove down the dirt road onto the paved highway. As we got out of sight of my family's home, my boyfriend, Curtis, who was hiding in the back seat of the car, sat up and we enjoyed a secret double date that evening. Curtis gave me a large beautiful brown teddy bear. I had just turned 16. It was an evening that I would always remember. But, I don't remember the movie that we saw.

We returned home after the movie and my sister and I got out of the car with the big brown teddy bear in my arms. My mom assumed that the teddy bear was a gift from my sister's boyfriend for my birthday. I didn't bother to correct her.

Curtis and I have been together since ninth grade and have been married since 1980 (over 28 years). I still have my big brown teddy bear that he gave me over 30 years ago, during the 70s. It has a special place in my heart and in our home. By the way, we just had enough nerve to tell my mom about that night we had the secret double date. She just laughed.

Re-Direction of a Guidance Counselor that Put Me on God's Path

I had the benefit of an incredible public education and wonderful teachers. It seemed that God had a way of putting special people (angels) in my life. Ms. Dees, the world's best history teacher, pulled me to the side while in high school and asked me if I was planning on being in her class the next school year. I was considering enrolling in the elite American Studies class that the top juniors traditionally attended. A lot of prestige and respect came with admittance in that special class. But, she urged me to enroll in her class where she could educate me on a different level and help me develop into the young lady whom she thought that I could be. She said, "Of course, you could be successful in that other class, but attend my class and you will experience history in a way that you will always remember."

I decided to take her advice and registered for her class. Some of my classmates and teachers were surprised that I had enrolled in the traditional history class rather than the elite class. But, this was a time when I chose to take a path that others may have considered not the best decision. After I agreed to register for Ms. Dees' history class, another teacher, Mrs. Wilson, approached me. These were both beautiful professional black women whom I admired. Mrs. Wilson asked me about the classes that I intended to take for the coming year and encouraged me to register to take her speech and drama class. She said that I had a terribly heavy southern accent. She indicated that there was nothing wrong with having a southern accent, but, she said that if I intended to travel beyond the borders of the south, I needed to re-learn how to speak and manage my accent. She said that she had heard that I was good in math and science, but commented that I may not be taken seriously as a scientist with a heavy southern accent. Wait a minute – what is it with my speech? I thought that I had overcome that problem in third grade. Oh my goodness, I feel like Moses with the speech impediment.

I registered for Mrs. Wilson's speech and drama class and Ms. Dees' history class. I must tell you that enrolling in those two classes required me to do more than earn A's. They wanted me to do more. As I excelled in both classes, I realized that these two women seemed to have more challenges in store for me. One day, as I was about to leave my history class, Ms. Dees asked me to stay after the students left, because she wanted to talk to me. She complimented me on how I dressed and conducted myself in class. She would always smile and compliment me in class. Then, she started telling me about two competitions that she believed I should consider participating in during my last two years of high school. She said that she wanted me to compete for Varsity Cheerleader and Azalea Trail Maid.

Even though these competitions are not typically successful for black students, she believed that I could compete and win. Both required high academic achievement and excellent communication skills. I told her I would talk it over with my mom and let her know. Now I knew why they were concerned about my speaking abilities. It wasn't just about my future. It was about my access to present experiences. I competed for both and was successful. I became a varsity cheerleader during my junior year and was an Azalea Trail Maid during my senior year. Both experiences added value to my life during those turbulent teen years, as I adapted into this emerging, newly reconciling society.

The Mobile Azalea Trail began in 1929, when citizens were encouraged to plant azaleas along the port city's thoroughfares. The blossom-lined streets became known as the Mobile Azalea Trail. High school seniors were selected to be apart of the Azalea Trail Court and served as hostesses for the official event when national and international dignitaries were invited to cut the ribbon to the official trail. Initially, the reigning Miss America served as Queen of the Azalea Trail which included Mobile native Yolanda Betbeze in 1951, and Lee Meriwether who later became an entertainment industry success in 1955.[6] Yolande Betbeze shocked pageant organizers and sponsors when she refused to wear a bathing suit in public. As a result of Ms. Betbeze's position, the swimwear sponsor withdrew its support and founded two rival beauty pageants, Miss USA and Miss Universe. Ms. Betbeze also marched in civil rights demonstrations, and took part in sit-ins in Woolworth's in New York.[7]

Lee Meriwether is probably best remembered for her role in the CBS television show "Barnaby Jones" and as Catwoman in the Batman series.

During this time, neighboring Jaycee chapters were invited to send representatives to serve in the Azalea Trail Court. The Azalea Trail Court grew in popularity to the point that other states were sending representatives. Eventually, the rules were changed to limit competition for the title of Azalea Trail Court to 50 senior girls selected from Mobile County Alabama high schools. Each girl competes for the title that includes having a minimum grade point average of 3.0. Evaluation criteria include their involvement in extracurricular activities, community involvement, completion of an application, answering various questions about their character, and interviewing before a panel of judges.

These 50 Azalea Trail Maids wear beautiful antebellum outfits, with no two looking alike and serve as "Official Ambassadors" to the city of Mobile.

The Azalea Trail Maids represent a symbol of Southern Hospitality.

The Mobile Jaycee's order all of the fabric that is involved with the main structure of the dress, so that all colors are uniform.

It is the Azalea Trail Maids responsibility to commission a dressmaker and come up with a design for her dress. Every Azalea Trail Maid dress is completely different because of this approach. The dressmaking process takes an average of three months for the dress to be completed. [8, 9]

A new program was started by the Mobile Jaycees that is known as America's Junior Miss Pageant, limited to out-of-town girls only.

The Azalea Trail Maids participated in the Obama January 20, 2009 Inaugural Parade.

My Azalea Trail Maid dress color was lavender.

Gail Mosley – Azalea Trail Maid, 1977

Transforming into Adulthood

I was preparing for the next phase of life – adulthood. I knew that any chance of success in life would require a college education. I would be the first in my family to attend college, so I didn't have anyone who had prior knowledge of how to handle the process or to give me advice. I only knew that my career would be in science – which was my passion.

I went to a guidance counselor and asked about the college process. She gave me a book and said to apply to the college or university that I wanted to attend. So, I went through the manual and picked out a few schools to apply to that had the major that I was seeking. One day, I was walking to class and Ms. Terry, one of the other guidance counselors, approached me. She asked me if I planned to attend college, I answered that I did. Then, she asked me which colleges was I planning on applying to and I told her Montevallo College and the University of Alabama. She stopped me and asked me to follow her. I went with her and she told me that I needed to go somewhere where I could heal and just enjoy the educational experience. She gave me some literature on a college in Alabama and told me to make sure that I visit their table when the college was scheduled to visit our school. She told me to ask about the possibility of receiving an academic scholarship at this specific college. I did as I was directed and received almost a complete academic scholarship to Talladega College, a historically black college, located in northeastern Alabama.

Talladega College is Alabama's oldest private historically black college, and is the home of the Amistad Murals. "There are three panels on the west wall of the library lobby representing *The Mutiny, The Court Scene, and The Return to Africa* that represent the Amistad Incident. A replica of the Amistad ship is embedded in the floor of the lobby. There is a tradition that no one walks on the ship's replica, because of its historic significance to the college.[10]

On the east wall are three panels representing *An Underground Railroad Scene, The Opening Day of School at Talladega College, and the Building of Savery Library.* The Amistad Murals have been exposed worldwide as historical treasures and Steven Spielberg's movie, *The Amistad,* has this incident as its subject.[11]

"The history of Talladega College began when two former slaves, William Savery and Thomas Tarrant, both of Talladega met with a group of new freedmen in Mobile, Alabama on November 20, 1865. As a result of the meeting they made a commitment, '...We regard the education of our children and youth as vital to the preservation of our liberties and true religion as the foundation of all real virtue, and shall use our utmost endeavors to promote these blessings in our common country.' Savery and Tarrant contacted General Wager Swayne of the Freedmen's Bureau about creating a school for the children of former slaves. As a result of their actions Talladega College was born which was initially a one-room schoolhouse. They used lumber salvaged from an abandoned carpenter's shop. The school overflowed with students. The school was expanded with the purchase of the Baptist Academy that was sold as a result of a mortgage default. The Baptist Academy had been built between 1852-53 with the help of slaves, including Savery and Tarrant. Savery and Tarrant contacted General Swayne who persuaded the American Missionary Association to purchase the building and 20 acres of land for $23,000. The building was renamed Swayne School, and it opened in November of 1867 with approximately 40 students. Thus, a building constructed with slave labor for white students became the home of the state's first college dedicated to servicing the educational needs of blacks."[12] When I arrived as a freshman, I was told that Talladega was an Underground Railroad location during slavery.

In the 1930s, Talladega College and other historically black colleges were the places where Jewish intellectuals, professors and scholars found acceptance after being expelled from prestigious German universities. Those Jewish refugees fled to America, but found their academic employment options limited by the religious and racial attitudes in this country. However, these brilliant academic professionals found that the historically black colleges welcomed them, and they became a part of that professional community, which included Talladega College in Alabama. Talladega College Jewish Professors included Julius Bobroff, William Hoffman, Fritz Pappenhein, Lore Rasmussen and Donald Rasmussen. A mutually beneficial bond was created by these two groups of people as a result of religious and racial barriers that existed at the time.

Those German Jewish refugees impacted the education of the black students in some of the historically black colleges.[13] They brought with them music, art and professional abilities that enhanced the academic experience of black students.[14] This historical contribution by immigrants benefited subsequent generations who attended institutions such as Talladega College, which included my generation.

My experience at Talladega College was what I needed to bandage my wounds of desegregation that I didn't even realize I had. I pledged in a sorority on that campus (Alpha Kappa Alpha). I achieved wonderful academic success and a different type of educational experience. I met Martin Luther King, Sr. during his visit to the campus. I met my first black female poet, Nikki Giovanni, in 1978. That year, I purchased a book of Nikki Giovanni's poetry titled, *Cotton Candy on a Rainy Day* during her visit to the Talladega College campus. I met her again on September 1, 2004 during her visit to Philadelphia, which was held at one of my favorite restaurants (Le Bec-Fin). My neighbor who worked for Smith Barney invited me to the special luncheon for "Women of Influence in Business, Society and Community." During her visit on September 1, 2004 I reminded her of her visit to Talladega College in 1978 and told her how she was the first poet whom I had ever met and how I treasured her poetry over the years. She gave me a big hug and autographed the book that I purchased in 1978. Twenty-six years had passed since our first meeting.

The college and professors seemed to realize that the students needed more than textbooks, lectures, exams, and formulas. We needed to see other people of color who were going before us, blazing the trail for us to follow. Martin Luther King, Sr. gave me a reflection of the sacrifices of the past and Nikki Giovanni provided me with a glimpse of future possibilities. I was educated at Talladega for two years, bandaged and repaired. I ultimately completed my undergraduate education at the University of Wisconsin-Madison.

Talladega College provided me with a place of refuge and encouragement that I desperately needed at that time in my life. There was one professor at Talladega College who inspires me to this day. Even though I was a biology major, I wanted to continue to work on speech. So, I registered for a Speech and Drama class. As I entered the classroom, I saw this beautiful woman sitting at the desk. I took a seat in class at a desk near the back of the room. She introduced herself and then got up from her desk and used two crutches to stand. She turned to write on the chalkboard and lectured until the class had almost come to an end. But, I guess she knew that the students were wondering about her condition.

As she sat back at her desk I could see the calluses on the inside of her beautiful hands. She then told us that she had dreamed of being an actress. But, she contracted polio only a few weeks before they found a cure for the dreaded disease. So, she wanted to make it clear that she tolerated no excuses from us who had the full use of our bodies. We had no excuse for failure, no reason to not pursue our dreams, because if she could find success in this life with her disease, we surely can find a way to be successful.

I would later hear from my former teacher almost 21 years later in 1998, after she saw my picture on the cover of *Black Enterprise Magazine*. She contacted me and told me that she lived in Maryland and that she was an artist.

The teachers in my life were God's angels. I listened to their wise counsel and respected their wisdom. Life was difficult enough, so avoiding unknown dangers at the direction of these people who cared so much was a blessing. Most of the teachers and professors in my life were demanding and firm, but they were also gentle and caring. For that gift of education, I will always be grateful.

Reconciliation – A Work in Progress

We were living in the Midwest. We had always attended all-black churches. We didn't know anything else. We had been raised in all-black churches and never considered anything else as a place to worship. My husband had attended an event in the Madison, Wisconsin area and came home very excited because the speaker was so incredible. He said that he heard that the speaker had a local church and he wanted us to consider attending. Then, he told me that the speaker was white. Well, needless to say I was hesitant to consider attending a non-black church or even visiting. I had never attended any church except black churches all my life. We were not welcomed at white churches in my community, so this was an unexpected request from my husband.

I was also concerned about being accepted in a non-black church. I didn't know if I could handle being rejected by Christians from another race. It may affect my relationship with God or change my attitude or make me feel differently, and I didn't want to risk it. Life was too hard and church was the only safe refuge that I had in life where I didn't have to deal with race, and I didn't want that refuge taken away from me.

Well, we had an intense discussion, but after hearing my husband talk about the message of that minister and seeing the excitement on his face, I finally agreed to possibly give it a try. But, he would have to go to the church alone to see if it was safe for our daughter and me to attend. He attended and came back even more excited than before. He told me that the church didn't have any black members, but he believed that we would be welcomed there.

"Oh no," I said to my husband, "I am not in any mood to go desegregate a church. That is one place that I can't deal with racial barriers. I can't worship in a stressful environment. I need to worship in an atmosphere of complete acceptance and tolerance, so that I experience a revival of my soul each Sunday, not oppression, stress or anxiety. If they don't have any black members, then I don't want to attend. I don't want to be responsible for any more desegregation – anywhere. Maybe they don't want black people in their church. Have you considered that possibility? I don't want to disrupt their worship environment, because of our presence. This is not public school. We shouldn't try to force people to include us in their community of worship."

But, he convinced me to attend and that was the best advice I have ever received. The name of the church was Capital City and it was affiliated with the Southern Baptist Association. So, we visited this local church that was being held in a school building not far from our home, and it was one of the best worship experiences in my life! They were some of the nicest people whom I had ever met in my life. Pastor Wood and his wife, Sandy, were magnificent teachers and became lifelong friends.

That was the most love I had ever experienced in my life from people of a different race. And guess what? – I didn't feel like I was black or Negro or African-American – I just felt like another Christian, another human, another one of God's creations. It was wonderful, it was invigorating, it was color-less worship, and it was liberating! It wasn't segregation (tolerating the presence of others into your community). It was my first step that began a lifelong process toward reconciliation for me. It was the first time in my life I was not rejected by the other race, but rather, embraced.

My time and the relationships built during the years we were members (the only black members mostly) were some of the best years of my life. I found healing for scars I didn't know that I had. I found acceptance, freedom and more importantly,

I found the presence of God in the midst of people who didn't look like me. There was no fear, no rejection, no hurt, and no pain. There was just an abundance of love and acceptance. I didn't know I could experience that on this earth in my lifetime. Curtis became the Worship Leader and we grew in ways that were not imaginable in our relationship with each other and in our relationship with other people of God from a different race. For the first time in my life, the color of my skin was irrelevant.

I also discovered that times had changed and progress in race relations had occurred. People of different races were beginning to mix voluntarily instead of by force. We were still living in the past. This new worship experience in this church allowed me to see and experience the progress in race relations from the front row of life. I also found that I became a part of the progress by my willingness to take a risk and worship with people who didn't look like me. This was the first moment of change in my life that was not bitter – no lemons this time, so no lemonade needed. The power of Christ had races, willingly, with love, and without pre-condition, worshipping and serving him together. Wow! I am experiencing acceptance while I am still young enough to enjoy it. Praise the Lord!

I hope that the presence of our family was as rewarding to the pastor, his wife and members of that church as it was to my family. It was a "win-win" relationship for all of us.

We had our first child, Courtney, before attending this church. We had our second child, our son, Brian, while attending the same church. My perceptions of people and my approach to life changed during those years. I began to realize how wonderful life could be if the different races could learn to live together on earth in harmony, instead of waiting until they get to heaven to try to learn to live together for all eternity.

If we had not followed God's direction to attend Capital City Church I would have probably never made the trip to Africa. Had we continued to attend a traditional African-American church, our daughter, in all likelihood, would not have developed a love for foreign missions. Traditional black churches have little or no emphasis on foreign missions because of the overwhelming demand to address local community needs and other priorities. Therefore, had we remained in that type of church, our daughter would not have had the Christian education inclusive of foreign missions that would lead her to the continent of Africa.

Dr. King said that the most segregated hour during the week is at 11:00 a.m. on Sunday mornings, during church service in this country. Even though progress has been made, we still have a long way to go as a nation. However, some Christian denominations have taken proactive steps toward healing the scars created as a result of our history. Such actions demonstrate that we are indeed healing as a nation and a people.

In 1995, the Southern Baptist Convention (SBC) took a proactive role in repudiating slavery and the role-played by the Southern Baptist Convention. This type of action by SBC would have probably had a major positive impact on the south and the institution of slavery, and probably my life as a child, if it had been taken when the need was greatest in this country. Nevertheless, the statement is still an important step in the reconciliation and healing process. I appreciate the SBC's actions as it reflects a social policy change in this religious organization.

SBC renounces racist past - Southern Baptist Convention

THE SOUTHERN Baptist Convention voted June 1995 to adopt a resolution renouncing its racist roots and apologizing for its past defense of slavery. On its opening day the convention altered its planned order of business in order to consider the statement of repudiation and repentance, prior to a celebration of the SBC's 150th anniversary the same evening. More than 20,000 Southern Baptists registered for the June 20-22 meeting at Atlanta's Georgia Dome.

The resolution declared that messengers, as SBC delegates are called, "unwaveringly denounce racism, in all its forms, as deplorable sin" and "lament and repudiate historic acts of evil such as slavery from which we continue to reap a bitter harvest." It offered an apology to all African-Americans for "condoning and/or perpetuating individual and systemic racism in our lifetime" and repentance for "racism of which we have been guilty, whether consciously or unconsciously." Although Southern Baptists have condemned racism in the past, this was the first time the predominantly white convention had dealt specifically with the issue of slavery.

The statement sought forgiveness "from our African-American brothers and sisters" and pledged to "eradicate racism in all its forms from Southern Baptist life and ministry." The SBC was founded in 1845 in Augusta, Georgia, by Baptists in the South seceding from the national Triennial Convention of Baptists after that body decreed it would not appoint slaveholders as missionaries. Currently about 500,000 members of the 15.6-million-member denomination are African-Americans and another 300,000 are ethnic minorities. Since 1980 most of the growth in Southern Baptist churches has been among racial and ethnic minorities. The racism resolution marked the denomination's first formal acknowledgment that racism played a role in its founding.[15]

CHAPTER 6

SUNSHINE

Fragmented memories…

Stay in the Sunshine by Showing Expressions of Love

The lyrics to a childhood song come to mind that has a lifelong message of joy, hope and happiness that is so true.

> You are my sunshine
> My only sunshine
> You make me happy
> When skies are blue
> You'll never know
> How much I love you
> You are my sunshine
> My only sunshine[16]

You know, we often forget about the awesome power of the beauty that surrounds us each day. One of the most precious gifts that God gave to all of us – equally – is the precious gift of sunshine (*some of us call it sunshine while others refer to it as sunlight*). Without sunshine, plants wouldn't grow and there would be no food to eat. Sunshine touches all of our lives, providing many physical and emotional benefits. It is cold outside, but I feel the warmth of the sunshine blazing through the windows. Sunshine provides us with our main source of vitamin D, which is believed to provide strength to our muscles and bones and boost our immune system.

Scientists believe that sunshine may even reduce your risk of cancer (breast, colon, ovary, bladder, womb, stomach, and prostate gland). Sunshine also makes you feel good emotionally. You just feel happier, your steps are a little peppier, your smile is bigger, and your attitude is more positive when it is sunny outside. Scientists believe that the sunshine cheers you up as a result of a chemical alteration, possibly preventing depression.[17, 18]

There is another form of sunshine that I experience that comes from my relationship with God. This sunshine shines even on a cloudy day. This sunshine shines within my soul and radiates to the outside. You may know what I am talking about. When things seem hopeless, and all seems lost, there is this calm and peace that you have that gives you strength from within. That kind of joy man can't give you and man can't take away. They can take away your dignity, your dreams, and your life, but they can't take away your loving relationship with God. It's the type of peace that you have in the midst of a storm. I didn't understand it as a child, but I understand it now.

I saw that internal sunshine in Uncle Preston and Grandma Eddie Mae when their oldest son was drafted into the army during the Vietnam War. The official orders confirmed that he was going to Vietnam. No one expected to see him again, because so many people were dying in that war, a war that seemed impossible to win. So, men just were sent away to die. He would be a low rank, so everyone expected him to be sent to the front line. But, Uncle Preston and Grandma Eddie Mae had inner peace, because they had prayed for a miracle that would save their son from the fate that was before him, out of his control, and out of their control, a fate decided by others. These others didn't know the needs of the family, and others didn't know my beloved cousin.

Seeing my cousin pick up a gun and kill someone was so foreign to this loving, kind and gentle young man. He was just beginning his young adult life. Having graduated from a segregated high school, he was attending a community college. He was like my brother, and my heart was heavy and sad. There was no sunshine in me that day. But, Uncle Preston and Grandma Eddie Mae were people of faith, and their prayers were answered, because my cousin's orders were changed and he was re-assigned to Germany. Praise be to God, my cousin was saved! I wrote him letters each week, while he was so far away, so he would get mail when names were called on the base.

But, life is like a revolving door. You are either coming out of a period of suffering (trial) or you are about to go into a period of suffering (trial). While my cousin was stationed in Germany, he had to return home because of an emergency. His younger brother, age 18, had been killed in a tragic car accident on a rainy night running an errand on behalf of the family. My cousin returned home from Germany. The day of the funeral approached. I hated funerals. I dreaded the days, as the date of the funeral grew closer.

Finally, that horrible day arrived. The family was seated on the front pews as close to the casket as possible. But, I slipped away from the family and found a place to sit as far back in the church as possible. OK, maybe if I close my eyes and put my fingers in my ears, I can make it through this day. I was shaking all over, my stomach churned, and sweat flowed down every part of my body under my clothing. I was so afraid. Lord, please don't let people start to cry, please don't let them sing those sad songs. Can't people just be quiet, so we can leave this place? I kept my eyes closed and my head down, as I hid between the pews.

Then I felt the touch of someone's arm around me. Oh no, it was Grandma Viola. Oh no, she is pulling me from between the pews. Then, she said the worst words that she ever spoke to me, "Come with me, Gail, so you can see your cousin for one last time." I answered, "I don't want to go up there. I don't want to see him like this. I want to remember him when we were together for the last time, watching cartoons and laughing in front of the TV, lying on the floor.

Please don't make me go. I am afraid. Please don't make me go!" But, nothing that I could say stopped the inevitable. I was taken to the casket and held up over his body, so I could see him one last time. My cousin's light skin looked white, and felt cold and unrecognizable.

That last glimpse of him haunted me for the rest of my life. If I close my eyes, I can still see him lying there in the casket.

After the funeral we all returned to Grandma Eddie Mae and Uncle Preston's house. Everyone was in black and people brought all this food and began to laugh and talk. What is wrong with these people? Don't they know that someone that I love just died? I don't want to eat, I don't want to laugh, I just want to be left alone, so I can grieve in my own way. Finally, that day ended. Grandma Eddie Mae asked if I was going to stay with her that night. I said, "Sure, Grandma, I wouldn't leave you alone." So, I stayed with her, as was typical for me, and she prepared the sofa cot for me to sleep on during the night.

Kenny and Peter were grieving, too. A few days had passed, so Kenny and Peter decided to go out to have a little fun, so they could get their minds off of the funeral. They were dressed in all-black leather that night, both looking handsome for the girls and ready for an evening away from the house. There was laughter during the evening as we commented on their very daring and bold attire. They left for the evening, looking good and feeling good.

Later that night, the telephone began to ring. The phone dropped and then I heard horrible words –

Kenny and Peter had been in a very bad car accident and they didn't know if either had survived. They called my dad, and he rushed to the hospital on their behalf. I heard them say that pieces of their leather outfits were lodged in the wheels of the tires. The car was totaled. Peter soon recovered, but Kenny was in a coma and was not expected to survive. Could this be happening? Will Uncle Preston lose both sons, both to car accidents so quickly? Grandma Eddie Mae and I began to cry. It was a cry of hopelessness and overwhelming grief.

But, Uncle Preston just left the room and went into the dining room and got on his knees and started to pray aloud. I always saw him get on his knees and pray beside his bed each night, but he always prayed silently, except at church. But, this prayer was different. He called out to God as a man filled with overwhelming grief. He pleaded with God to save his last son. He pleaded with God not to take both of his sons from him. He begged and pleaded with God, sobbing profusely which seemed like all night.

It seemed like the room was caving in on me. It was all too difficult to handle. This burden was too great to handle for our family. Then, he got up off his knees and he looked at us with a type of peace and confidence that I had never seen before. He said to us that God was not going to take his son; God was not going to take Kenny home – not yet. Grandma Eddie Mae said, "OK." She instantly stopped crying and began to prepare food. She seemed as calmed and relaxed as Uncle Preston did. Because they felt so confident, I felt better, too. Kenny was not going to die. I trusted them and they trusted God, and that was enough for me. I didn't understand it all, but somehow I felt much better. They had that internal sunshine again. So, I went to my cot and slept peacefully through the night.

The next day, my dad brought back grim news. Kenny was in a coma on life support in the intensive care unit at the hospital. They didn't expect him to make it. Uncle Preston instructed him and the rest of the family to keep around the clock watch over Kenny, and to not allow anyone to take the life support off of him. They scheduled shifts, so that Kenny was never alone. He was in intensive care, for a long time, with no signs of gaining consciousness. Finally, doctors told the family that he was brain dead and his life support should be removed. The family refused. Later, they were told that they could no longer keep him on life support in the hospital. Immediately, the family started looking for locations to transfer Kenny that would not remove his life support. They found a nursing home. He was moved to the nursing home and he stayed on life support, in a coma for several years. He was the youngest person in the nursing home.

He was in his early 20s.

Another one of life's lemons.

While You Were Sleeping

I was scheduled to stay with Kenny on weekends and sometimes after school. The family members aided in the care of Kenny, including me. We bathed him, fed him through his feeding tube, turned his body, so he wouldn't get bed sores (the family purchased a sheep skin for him to protect his body), put lotion on him, emptied his urine from the bag, and exercised his legs and arms. I treated his body like it was mine, and so did every other family member who worked the shifts. He was kept clean, groomed and in excellent physical condition. I did a lot of things that the nurses did. But, I also did other things – I read to him, and talked to him constantly. In fact, I talked so much that it drove the other people in the room crazy. I would sing to him too, even though I am not a good singer. In fact, I am a horrible singer. The family continued their 24-hour watch over Kenny for what seemed like years. I don't remember exactly how long, but it was a long time – at least to me.

Then, one day, the sun was shining brightly. I was in the room with him that day looking out the window and just enjoying the sunshine. Then, I heard this voice. I turned and looked and Kenny was looking straight at me with his eyes wide open. Then, I heard him speak. I jumped and screamed. The nurses came into the room and they saw that he was alert and they heard him speak.

The family was excited and so happy, because Kenny was out of his coma. Later, his feeding tubes were removed and he began the long road to recovery, beginning with physical therapy. Uncle Preston's prayer was answered. He had faith in God that his prayer would be answered. His wife and the family trusted his faith in God, and their actions over the years were based on the faith of this man that

94

God would save his oldest and last son. Observing his faith in God resulted in my unwavering trust in God. I learned a lifelong lesson: When faced with bad circumstances in life (lemons) it doesn't mean that God is not with you. Your circumstances do not mean that God doesn't love you. He will answer your prayers and bless you right where you are. It also taught me that faith is not "inactive or passive" but rather active, engaging and believing.

Kenny spent years in recovery and had to learn how to talk and walk again. We also had to bring him up to date on what he had missed while he was sleeping.

CHAPTER 7

COMMUNITY IN CRISIS – THE LANDFILL

Fragmented memories...

Well, if life were not difficult enough with my daily struggles with coping with desegregation, another battle emerged that would forever change my young life. Our community was identified as a location for a landfill, and it was going to be placed directly across the road from where my family lived, just a few hundred yards from our mailbox. This is directly in front of where I caught the bus each day, on the land where we used to farm soybeans and gather our harvest with the large "combine tractor" that I used to ride in with my dad. It was a battle that would overshadow my childhood and my adulthood. It was a battle that would be the final decider of who and what I would become professionally. The career that I would pursue didn't even exist yet in the universities and colleges – environmentalist.

As my life continued to be changed by others, all that change came with an ocean of pain.

An Ocean of Pain
For every mountain…
For every valley…
For every disappointment…
For every struggle…
GOD has brought me through and for that I give him the praise!

This time, I experienced the hurt that can be inflicted upon an entire community. Another lemon in my life. This was a small farming community. Everyone's daily survival depended upon getting clean water from the drinking water wells on their property. The wells were shallow. There was no public water, no public sewage or other public services in our community, except for electricity. There was no storm water drainage system. We all had well water and septic systems. This was also a hurricane area and floods from heavy rains and storms are a way of life for us in this Gulf Coast Region. What will happen to us? This will destroy our quality of life and the ability for us to even have clean water to drink. We had been workers of the land since our ancestors became sharecroppers for former slave-owners at the end of the Civil War. We have earned our right to be here. This is all we know, and this is all we have. This land is our survival.

Why us? Well, we knew the answer to that question. After all, they were placing the landfill in the heart of a small working class, primarily black community. Yes, there were a few white families who lived in the community, but they likely had the resources to sell their homes and move. Our community was made up of mostly farmers and domestic labor: housekeepers, cooks and janitors. The few professionals in our community were teachers.

I helped my Grandma Eddie Mae clean houses. She would pick up the small wages for the day off of the kitchen table at the house that we cleaned. There would be a few dollar bills and coins on the table. (I would get the coins).

I come from a family of cooks, who used those skills to make money to help feed the family. The black people in the community couldn't afford to move anywhere. Even if they wanted to move, what would they get for the homes in a community where a landfill was going to be located. The land was all they had. The land was all my family had. The beautiful environment – my angel, my friend was going to be taken away. "Don't you love us Lord? Don't you care about our plight in life? Don't you hear our cries? You heard the cries of the Israelites as referenced in the Old Testament in Exodus. It is our only economic livelihood." It was the only thing of value that we could pass on to the next generation. It was our only legacy.

The rules of the game for the powerful are to identify a vulnerable community – typically minority and poor – and then, place the polluting sources in locations where the people are too weak to fight.

But, I have learned through life's lessons that God is the final decider, so we should never forget the source of our strength and salvation. If you believe that God can save you after you die, so that you will go to heaven – you know – the big stuff. Well, can't you believe that he can handle a person hell-bent on doing evil – you know – the little stuff?

My father organized support in the community and churches to fight the placement of the landfill. They combined their limited resources to try to fight the destruction of our community. My father found an attorney and technical experts to help us. That was a difficult challenge. It was a black attorney who agreed to fight on behalf of our community. I will never forget his name – Michael A. Figures.

Michael A. Figures would later become the first African-American elected to the Alabama State Senate from Mobile County. Senator Michael A. Figures was elected in 1995 as President *Pro Tempore* of the Senate by an overwhelming majority of his colleagues who made him the highest-ranking African-American in Alabama State government.

When I was a child, attorney Figures' legal representation was indeed a blessing to our community. But, we still needed an expert to generate the data to defend our position. No one would help us. My dad identified professionals to generate the data needed to defend the case. As a result, the case was dismissed in favor of our community. The placement of the land-fill in the community was defeated. But, the process drained the financial resources of our family and our community. It was a difficult battle and it came with a price. The days, weeks and months of anxiety that engulfed our home robbed me of days, weeks and months of joy. The stress of the battle had taken an emotional toll on me, when combined with all the other battles waging in my life. It was too much for too young a mind.

Years later, that community and my family would have to fight again to try to keep a polluting source out of the community on that same land. I was living in Wisconsin at the time and received a call for help. I flew to Alabama and appeared in court as an expert witness. But, the judge had no desire to deny the powerful party representing the cotton gin his victory against our community. The community lost the case – no victory. This would be the ultimate insult to our black community – a Cotton Gin – a daily reminder of our role during slavery. We would be forced to remember the horrible past that we thought we had overcome. It was a sad day for me when the judge allowed the placement of a Cotton Gin across the street from the home where I grew up. This was a lemon that I did not turn into lemonade. But, after that court decision, I decided to become an environmental attorney.

I never knew until recently why I became a biologist, environmentalist and attorney. It wasn't until I was on that plane landing in Africa that I realized why I had become the woman that I am. I had received a greeting card from someone from my home church in Alabama after I completed law school. The card congratulated me on my accomplishments, but also stated the following, "Now we have our own!" As I remembered the card, I understood the message.

The career choices that I had made were directly related to my desire to remove those things in my life and the life of the community that I grew up in that made me feel powerless. I knew how hard the community had to struggle to get people to represent them – so my being an attorney, biologist and environmentalist appeared to remove the community's vulnerability. No matter where I lived, they knew that I would always be there for them. I would come to their support, equipped with the knowledge of science, the environment, the law, and the BIBLE! I cried when I realized where my Journey of Pain (my lemons) had led me. It was all part of God's master plan for my life. Who was better equipped to fight the environmental battle than someone who had to rely on the environment during those harsh initial years of school desegregation?

CHAPTER 8

THE WIZARD OF OZ SYNDROME

You hear all your life that if you work hard, get an education and do your best, you can experience the American Dream. So, you have the beginning and the end of the story, but what about that all-critical middle of the story? You know, the part where all the pain and suffering occurs trying to gain access to experience the American Dream.

The Beginning of the Story

You are born in a family, in a place chosen by others, destined to begin a life based upon the conditions of others. But, you inherit more than their genetics, you inherit their social status in our society that comes pre-packaged with obstacles and pre-set limitations.

As a child, you may not recognize your position in life and how it may impact your hopes and dreams. As you get older, you begin to recognize your surroundings, and as you discover who you are, you also begin to discover potential limitations in your life. This is most obvious with the poor and homeless in society. Daily survival is the priority, not education that is the foundation required to make your hopes and dreams a reality. Initially, you begin to observe the experiences of the people in your circle of life – their joys, their pains, their struggles, their successes, their failures and their obstacles. But, you are still on the outside looking in, because you are too young to comprehend it all, and you have not entered the next phase of life that leads to the middle of the story.

Then it happens! An awful thing happens, you find out that whom and what you are is determined by how society views your race, gender, appearance, and other factors that you have no control over. You realize that you have been born into a "social and economic rut" in life that you are destined to live in for the rest of your life, unless you figure a way out.

The End of the Story

Then, you jump to the end of the story, which by the way sounds familiar to the beginning of the story. If you had worked hard, gotten an education, and did your best, you would have experienced the American Dream. It's your own fault that you failed, because everyone has access to the American Dream.

Well, that may not be exactly true – at least not for everyone.

What Happened in the Middle of the Story?

What happened to Dorothy when she arrived at Emerald City, knocked on the door after traveling so far, following the explicit directions of the "Good Witch" whom she trusted and relied upon for truth, wisdom and direction so she could get to the right destination and find her way home? She was put on a yellow brick road (the first step you take to begin the middle of the story – *life's journey*). Having entered the forest that looked fearful and dangerous (*the world of competition – whatever profession you choose to pursue*), she took on the obstacles of life, fighting off attacks against her and the people she loved, including her beloved pet "Toto." (*Side note: Hey, we all need a Toto in our life. My Toto's name is Buttercup, a beautiful Beagle and faithful companion over the years. Well, let's get back to the story.*)

Evolution of the Soul

As I look back on my life, I see a pattern of "pain to gain" embodying a life of long-suffering. My favorite song is by Mary Mary with the lyrics reflecting the pain in life that I have had to endure.

The lyrics express what I feel inside:

Shackles (Praise You)

Whoo! It sure is hot out here - Ya know? I don't mind thought - Just glad to be great - Know what I'm saying, uh!

Take the shackles off my feet so I can dance I just wanna praise you (What'cha wanna do?) I just wanna praise you.

You broke the chains now I can lift my hands (Uh feel me?) And I'm gonna praise you. (What'cha gon do?) I'm gonna praise you.

In the corners of mind I just can't seem to find a reason to believe that I can break free. Cause you see I have been down for so long - feel like the hope is gone. But as I lift my hands, I understand that I should praise you through my circumstance.

Take the shackles off my feet so I can dance. I just wanna praise you. I just wanna praise you.

You broke the chains now I can lift my hands. And I'm gonna praise you, I'm gonna praise you.

Everything that could go wrong all went wrong at one time. So much pressure fell on me - I thought I was gonna lose my mind.

But I know you wanna see if I will hold on through these trials. But I need you to lift this load, cause I can't take it anymore.

Take the shackles off my feet so I can dance. I just wanna praise you, I just wanna praise you.

You broke the chains now I can lift my hands, and I'm gonna praise you - I'm gonna praise you. Been through the fire and the rain, bound in every kind of way, but God has broken every chain, so let me go right now.

Take the shackles off my feet so I can dance. I just wanna praise you, I just wanna praise you.

You broke the chains now I can lift my hands - And I'm gonna praise you, I'm gonna praise you…

The Journey to Emerald City

When I was born, doors were already closed to me. Those doors had been closed for generations. Many in society tried to correct past wrongs by fighting in the civil war to end slavery, and by official acts by those who represented the leadership in our society during various periods of time in history. The Emancipation Proclamation freeing slaves, the 13th Amendment intended to wipe out the final reminisces of slavery, the 14th Amendment granting equal protection to the newly freed Negro slaves, the court ruling in Brown v. Board of Education overturning the "separate but equal" doctrine of Plessy v. Ferguson, and the enactment of the Civil Rights Act, intended to destroy the racial barriers created under years of Jim Crow segregationist laws. All these actions worked to create a more perfect union in our country. The sacrifices made by others in the past created a foundation that would make my journey possible in my lifetime, providing me with a better future than those who lived in previous generations. No government is perfect, but this society has evolved into a more free society over time, overcoming national struggles to arrive at this point in time in our nation's history. A time that we should be proud to be a part of for those of us experiencing 21st century America.

The journey to Emerald City for me meant that I had to walk the yellow brick road of life that I was born into. I did all the things that I was told would give me the best opportunity for success and obtained the education that I was told would be the key to the door of Emerald City. But, I would soon find out that my key didn't fit the lock to the door to Emerald City. I had to knock on the door and request permission to enter.

Battle for a Professional Career

After graduation from college, I knew that I had to obtain a professional job immediately in order to pay for my education. I knew that it would be a difficult road ahead, but I was prepared to work hard to obtain my first professional job. The first job interview that I had was in the private sector. My hopes were immediately shattered when the person conducting the interview told me that he didn't think that I was "mechanically inclined," so he couldn't offer me the job. What a sexist remark. Just because I am a woman I could not be mechanically inclined. I tried to convince the gentleman performing the interview that I was indeed mechanically inclined. I explained to him that my father didn't have any sons – so I was his right hand girl – I worked at the service station – so I could fix a tire and change my own oil, fix a broken water hose if my car broke down, I could diagnose mechanical problems with your vehicle. I grew up getting my hands dirty. I explained to him that my gift from my dad when I went off to college was some tools and spare parts to repair my car if I broke down on the road. I was definitely mechanically inclined. I explained to him that my dad was gifted to do many things and I learned from him many things that a typical girl may not have been exposed to.

Why does being a woman automatically disqualify me for the job because you don't consider females mechanically inclined? "Please, sir – give me a chance. Please don't hold being a woman against me. I need the job. I need the money. I need to pay back my student loans." I didn't get the job. Being a female was not a good thing to be on that day at the door of Emerald City.

No open door in the private sector for this college graduate. It seemed that my gender was more of an issue. They didn't seem to care about my race. What? Do you mean that I have to worry about gender now to get a job? I was not prepared for that battle. I had learned to fight the racial battle, I didn't realize that there was a gender battle, too. So, I discovered that I had the female key to Emerald City, which didn't fit the lock to the door.

I returned home discouraged and worried. Who was going to give me a chance to begin my professional career? My husband was working at the Urban League at that time and knew that my heart was broken. He wanted to help and told me to contact this very nice gentleman who may be able to tell me about employment opportunities at the state. I contacted him (Fred was his name) and eventually I gained a project employment position with the state. It was just temporary, short-term employment, but at least it was a start, while I continued to look for a full-time permanent job. It was a great position, working in Natural Resources, dealing with wildlife and natural area issues within the state, which resulted in my first professional publication. But, I couldn't get comfortable in that temporary position that may last for only a few months. I had to try to find permanent professional employment.

While working in the temporary position for the state I met an angel whose name was Dannette (a member of the Delta Sigma Theta Sorority), who worked in the Department of Natural Resources (DNR). She had a permanent job and said that she would show me how to prepare and study for the state exams so I would have an opportunity for employment. I eventually got my first full-time job with the State of Wisconsin. Dannette was Catholic and a wonderful person. She was such a good friend that I named my daughter after her by making my daughter's middle name Dannette.

Three Strikes against You – You're Black, a Woman and a Mother

My husband wanted to move back to Alabama, but I really wanted to stay in Wisconsin. My career was going wonderfully, I had great friends, a wonderful church, and lived in a wonderful city. I had gotten comfortable in this new life in this different part of the country. I loved living in that beautiful city on an isthmus between the two lakes. But, Curtis really missed living at home near his family, so we decided to pursue moving back to Alabama. Our résumés were given to headhunters, and it was agreed that if either one of us got the first job in our hometown in Alabama, we would move. Traditional gender roles would not be a factor. It wouldn't matter whether I got the job first or he got the job first. It was agreed that I wouldn't have to deal with that male ego stuff. We were equally gifted and talented and there was no need for one of us to be threatened by the success of the other. Life was too hard for both of us to bother with that type of trivial stuff. The couples that have time to fight over gender roles must have had it easier in life than we have, because that isn't even in our vocabulary. If a door opens for either one of us, just hurry up and run through that door before the door closes. Get there in time, so one of us can hold the door open for the other spouse to get through. That's where it starts and that's where it ends! Gender conversation over — next issue in life, please.

As it worked out, I received the first job offer as a scientist for an engineering firm in Alabama. During the interview with the company leadership, I was asked if I had become a "damned Yankee" living in the North. I said, "No sir, I will always be a Southern Belle." Then, I was asked whether I still remembered my place and where the lines were, and I answered, "Yes sir." This was in the mid-80s.

I later received a job offer and we moved back home to Alabama. My husband didn't have a job yet, but found professional employment quickly after we arrived, and we started our new jobs around the same time.

I was not excited to make the move back south, but being close to family was so important to my husband and our families. But, for me, I wanted my children to grow up in the Midwest and experience a different type of life. Also, I would miss the Broadway shows that would come through Madison as they passed through the Chicago area. I would miss the beautiful city where I had spent so many wonderful years. I would miss the church and new friends I had made. I would also miss my best friend, Spring, who still lives in Wisconsin, and her daughters (of which the oldest is my Goddaughter).

We moved back home and joined my husband's family church. But, things were different. I really missed Madison. I missed the diversity, inclusiveness, and the being with a broader group of people on a social level. We could go to dinner with people from different races. But, at home, the race relationship didn't seem to have evolved much since we had left. The races still didn't interact on a social level. I guess Curtis was missing the social diversity, too, because he said that he was open to leaving his family church and joining a mixed church.

We later joined Cottage Hill Baptist Church, because they allowed blacks to become members some years before and the pastor was a good speaker. But, it did not have that same "colorless" feeling of acceptance and inclusion as the church in Madison. Also, my joining Cottage Hill Baptist Church was not well received by an administrative staff person at the engineering firm where I was working. She was an older woman, maybe the age of my grandmother. She told me that she was against the desegregation of Cottage Hill Baptist Church (a Southern Baptist Church) and some members left the church after they made the decision to desegregate. That statement brought back memories of the past that I didn't care to remember. Things hadn't changed as much as I had hoped. Things were very much the same.

During our time in Alabama, we returned to the traditional ruts of social and religious separateness. We didn't make any new friends who were not black to include in our circle of life. It was like going to a desegregated school in the 60s and 70s – you have both races in the audience, but you don't become friends or interact outside of that organized group setting. Your social lives have no interaction outside of school or work. You don't go to dinner, get invited to parties, movies or baby showers together. For the most part, the lives of the black community and the lives of the white community hadn't really changed much over time. We discovered they were still mostly separate when we moved back to Alabama. Even Mardi Gras was still segregated. The only social life we had was with relatives. This re-adjustment was difficult, because I had grown to enjoy the broader relationships and diversity. Now, that was normal for me – not being separate.

But, we were here, so let's make the best of it, so I decided to focus on work and prove my worth to the engineering firm by coming up with something unique that would provide them with a competitive edge in the industry nationally. So, I performed independent research and came up with an approach that I presented to the Vice President of the firm.

My professional strength was in environmental regulatory analysis as a result of experience gained working for the State of Wisconsin. I identified an expansion opportunity for the firm that would provide them with a competitive edge in a newly emerging environmental compliance area. The Vice President loved my idea and told me to use the resources of the company to execute the concept. I was successful. There was a special dinner to celebrate the benefits that would be experienced by the company as a result of my efforts. I received special recognition and many thanks for my vision and hard work to the benefit of the firm. I was happy and very excited. Hard work can make a difference.

A few weeks passed and then I received a phone call from a friend at the U.S Environmental Protection Agency (U.S. EPA) office in Atlanta. He called to warn me, because he had had a very disturbing conversation with the Assistant Vice President of the Firm that I was working for. He said that his heart grieved for me, because of what they were about to do to me. He then told me that they were going to hire a white male to take over the program that I had developed and obtained U.S. EPA accreditation for. I would not receive the benefit of all my hard work. He offered to help me get a job at U.S. EPA and my family could move to Atlanta, but I told him it would be unfair to my family to move them again when we just moved from Wisconsin to Alabama. I thanked him for caring enough to call.

My heart was broken. I don't remember how long I cried, but it was for a long time. I had grown tired of fighting and I was fed up trying to turn the lemons in my life into lemonade. Why do so many things in my life have to be a struggle? I prayed all night and cried until I fell asleep. This time, I didn't believe that I would have the strength to overcome this struggle. I couldn't think of any way to turn this lemon into lemonade. I was finally defeated. There was nothing to do, but to prepare myself emotionally, so I could endure the blow of the loss. My key to Emerald City was about to be given to someone else.

My mind raced as I drove to work the next morning. My heart was heavy. I had no joy, no strength, and no hope. I was even too broken to pray or cry anymore. I was numb!

I finally arrived in the parking lot. That seemed like a long drive to work on that particular day. I entered the building, went to my desk, and stayed to myself most of the day. Finally, it was time for our lunch break. I could get out of this building and breathe the fresh air, look at the beauty of the environment, and admire the cloud formations. The environment always relaxed me and seemed to give me hope. I could smell the fresh roasted peanuts in the air that baked at the local nut shop, located only a short distance from where I worked. But, I had no appetite. I felt sick and was overwhelmed with nausea. What is wrong with me? I don't remember having this much anxiety before with other difficult experiences in my life.

I went back to work after my lunch break, with an empty stomach, and waited until I would get the news. Maybe they don't intend to tell me today. Maybe they are reconsidering and will change their minds. But, a few minutes later, I was called into the office of the Vice President. He was polite, as usual, but didn't offer me a seat. He just politely informed me that I would be getting a new boss. "Someone to take over the program by the horns you developed for the company. But, we did you a favor. We hired a Yankee to be your boss. He's a good guy and we think that you will like him."

I was silent. He looked at me, waiting on a response, but I said nothing. He then said, "Honey, you know that you can't ever be a manager in this firm. Look around you. Besides, I know it must be difficult for you, but face it, you have **three strikes against you – You're black, you're female and you're a mother."** I said, "Thank you for the information," and then left his office. Wow! That was a lot of lemons! Wait a minute – I am the lemon this time!

He was right. The Yankee from the Midwest was a wonderful guy. If I had to work for anyone, I would have chosen him. So, in their own twisted way, they tried to reward me by hiring someone from a part of the country that would treat me better than someone currently in the company in that office. I had already been warned, so I was at peace and knew that somehow God would come to my rescue. I didn't know what God would do or how God would do it, but I knew that I had come too far in my life to be left in these circumstances. I had worked too hard for this to be the end of my professional career.

Then, I ran into the Assistant Vice President in the hallway. He stopped to talk to me about things going on in the company and what my options were. We were co-authoring a couple of articles for news print publication. He is the one who told my friend at U.S. EPA what was about to happen to me. I listened to what he had to say. He responded to me with a question, – "What are you going to do? Move your young family again? I know the people in charge where your husband works. I know someone on the board of the commission that you would file a complaint with, if that is the road that you decide to take." I didn't respond. I just listened, because there was really nothing that I could say. I was trapped, defeated and stuck to work for them in the position and status that they dictated for me. I had better be a good little girl, because it seemed that all the possible alternatives that I may have, had already been evaluated by them and I was defeated in their eyes and in my heart.

Oh, if that wasn't enough to deal with, I found out that I was pregnant with my third child after using a home pregnancy test later that night. That explains why I felt so sick with nausea. But, that really limits my options. As I shared things with Curtis, he seemed lost for words to say to me that would give me any form of encouragement. But, somehow I wasn't worried. I had seen miracles in the past resulting from prayer. So, I just prayed to God for a miracle. I didn't want to work for the firm anymore, because I couldn't do my best for a company that would hurt me this way. But, I didn't get angry. I just knew God was going to make a way out of no way for me. I started to wait for the ingredients from God, so I could make lemonade out of these lemons. I was not in the mood for change and I definitely was not in the mood to make any lemonade out of this large batch of bitter lemons. Some sweetness from God to make some lemonade was my only option at this point. The company seemed firm in their decision and I had no apparent options.

I got dressed and drove to work the next morning. A few days passed.

One day, the telephone rang in my office. It was the University of Wisconsin, Department of Engineering. It was Mr. Waxman. He was very upset because the curriculum that I had written and gotten U.S. EPA accredited for the engineering firm I was working for refused to allow others access to the training. The firm rejected the request of the University of Wisconsin to have access to the program that I had created. I was aware of only two U.S. EPA accredited asbestos project designer programs in the country at the time: the one in Kansas and the one at the engineering firm that I had created. However, all professionals around the country would be required to obtain the U.S. EPA accredited training, in order to perform those types of services under the new federal law. It seemed that I had created a business monopoly for my firm and they refused to share their golden egg that I had provided to them on a silver platter.

Then the words came from the mouth of Mr. Waxman (my angel, my ingredient to make lemonade out of another one of life's lemons) that changed my life forever. Those words made a way out of no way for me. The doors had been closed, but God opened a window for me to enter. Mr. Waxman said, "What about you working for the University of Wisconsin as a consultant and developing a U.S. EPA accredited program for us? Gail, this is your chance to start your own business. Just tell us what you need and we will do it." I told them I just wanted a 50% cash advance and I would write the program for them, get the program accredited and be prepared to teach the first courses after the birth of my baby. So, the soonest I could get to Wisconsin to teach would be February the following year since my baby was due in November.

I went home and told my husband that I intended to quit my job and start my own environmental engineering and consulting firm. I guess he thought that all the stress of the situation had made me delirious. So he told me, "That's fine, honey, and you can just keep the money you make as spending change." I spent a portion of the money to buy a computer and start my business working out of my home. My *alma mater*, The University of Wisconsin – Madison provided me with the seed money to start my own business and create a new life for my family and me. Boy, this would be the best and longest lasting jar of lemonade that I would make. That jar of lemonade, which was made in March 1988, has lasted for over 20 years.

I met my schedule and obtained U.S. EPA accreditation for the program that I created for the University of Wisconsin and started instructing the course the following February, as I had promised, after my last child, Daniel, was born. I commuted from Alabama to Wisconsin in the winter to perform the second component of my first contract. What an unexpected blessing with my first contract coming from my *alma mater*. That was the last time I worked for someone else as a full-time employee in my life. For the rest of my career, I would be a self-employed business owner, an entrepreneur.

I turned my obstacles into stepping stones. When I was given lemons in life I made lemonade with whatever sweet blessing God would send my way. Similar to my career being an evolution of my life experience, not something that I picked out of a college catalog, so was the creation of my business. No business plan, no bank loan, no partner, no investor, no government agencies to tell me what to do or how to do, just me and my first client and the rest is history. Whatever the outcome, the true answer is that God turned something bad into something good.

Jesus' torment and ultimate death on the cross was something that was bad, but the ultimate outcome resulted in something for the good of all mankind. As a result of his resurrection, his pain resulted in our gain. We gained an opportunity for salvation as a result of his crucifixion on the cross. His shed **blood** paid the price for the redemption of our sins.

I resigned from the firm that caused me pain. But I left quietly, respectfully and professionally. They didn't even know that I was pregnant or had started my own business. This was one of those times when I heeded my mother's advice, "You win your best battles with your mouth shut." So, I never said a word. This time, I wasn't supposed to fight back. I let them think that they had won the victory and I moved on.

I don't believe in burning bridges, even though you can't do anything when someone burns a bridge that you are using to gain access to maintain your economic livelihood. So, even though the firm hurt me, they called me back as a consultant after I resigned. I accepted the brief assignment. They needed an approved U.S. EPA instructor and it was inappropriate to hurt them just because they hurt me.

I began to try to market my business in the local area where I was living in Alabama, but the presence and power of my former employer, and all their local connections and influence didn't seem to allow me to gain access to local contracts. Relocation seemed to provide the best option to have a chance to survive as a new small business owner.

The Move Northeast

We didn't stay in the south very long. We moved when my husband's employer offered him a job opportunity on the East Coast. That would be our last move.

Years later, the Vice President of that firm where I had worked asked to meet with me at their Northeastern Pennsylvania office. He apologized to me and expressed his regret for the mistake of not valuing my gifts and talents. I told him that I held no malice against him or the company and that I forgave him for his actions and words on the day that he spoke to me. I told him that God had provided for my needs in spite of my circumstances, and that I didn't care to look back to the past, but rather forward to the future of possibilities. I knew when I interviewed for the job at the engineering firm that all the company leadership was all white males. I thought that if I shocked them with my abilities that I could overcome those obstacles. I gave it my best and failed, and eventually had to move in a different direction for my career and my life. I wanted him to know that I had forgiven him. That day allowed us both to experience forgiveness, reconciliation and healing.

So, this is a portion of the middle of my story. This reflects a portion of my journey along the yellow brick road in life, trying to gain access to the Emerald City (the land of economic opportunity). I tried to follow the directions of those angels (unexpected friends and good people) God placed in my life. I tried to fight off the wicked witches who would light matches to set me on fire to try to destroy my very existence and interrupt my journey. Sometimes, I would skip and sing, and sometimes, I would run and cry, while pleading to God for the strength to make it through another day. I used to think that my crying was a sign of weakness. But, then, I remembered that Jesus cried, too. In John chapter 11, verse 35, it says that, "Jesus wept," because he was overcome by the mourning being experienced by those he loved.

John 11:21-35

[21]"Lord," Martha said to Jesus, "if you had been here, my brother would not have died.

[22]But I know that even now God will give you whatever you ask."

²³Jesus said to her, "Your brother will rise again."

²⁴Martha answered, "I know he will rise again in the resurrection at the last day."

²⁵Jesus said to her, "I am the resurrection and the life. He who believes in me will live, even though he dies;

²⁶and whoever lives and believes in me will never die. Do you believe this?"

²⁷"Yes, Lord," she told him, "I believe that you are the Christ, the Son of God, who was to come into the world."

²⁸And after she had said this, she went back and called her sister Mary aside. "The Teacher is here," she said, "and is asking for you."

²⁹When Mary heard this, she got up quickly and went to him.

³⁰Now Jesus had not yet entered the village, but was still at the place where Martha had met him.

³¹When the Jews who had been with Mary in the house, comforting her, noticed how quickly she got up and went out, they followed her, supposing she was going to the tomb to mourn there.

³²When Mary reached the place where Jesus was and saw him, she fell at his feet and said, "Lord, if you had been here, my brother would not have died."

³³When Jesus saw her weeping, and the Jews who had come along with her also weeping, he was deeply moved in spirit and troubled.

³⁴"Where have you laid him?" he asked. "Come and see, Lord," they replied.

³⁵Jesus wept.

So, it's OK if you weep as you travel along your life's journey, trying to arrive at your final destination. Whatever your Emerald City is, just never allow others to take you off your journey. Keep on walking, keeping your load light, not carrying the burden of anger, hatred or bitterness with you, so you will be able to complete the journey intended just for you. Remember, God loves you and is watching out for you – even when you don't think or know he is looking.

Basket Full of Eggs

Because of my life experiences, I tend to willingly explore new approaches and live outside the box. I had trusted God completely by faith in 1988 to start a business and he has met my family's needs as a result of that leap of faith.

I had asked my husband to join me in the business for over seven years, but the answer was always the same, "No." One day, I asked my husband again, "Why won't you join in the business with me?" His response was that he didn't want to put all his eggs in one basket. His corporate job gave him the type of security that he relied upon for our family. My response to him was, "So, you don't trust God to hold the basket with all the eggs? You trust man over God to meet your needs?" After that interaction, he left corporate America and joined the company, and we have had all our needs met.

It hasn't been easy. We haven't had the financial success that we could have achieved, because of so many closed doors and locked windows. But, God has never failed us. He has met our needs for clothing, housing, education of our children, and he has always allowed me to do my Valentine's Ball each year for about twelve years for the teenagers. It has allowed us to see our children grow up that would not have been possible if we worked traditional jobs. Soccer games, ballet practice, guitar practice, school musicals, school events, and volunteering have never been an issue for us. God's gift to us was not financial gain, but time with our children (and their friends) that is more precious than any amount of money to me.

By the way, if I trust God for the big thing (*saving us for eternity after death*), can't I trust him with the little things *(holding ALL our eggs)*?

126

CHAPTER 9

TEA CAKES

I don't know what our family roles were during slavery. We lack pre-Civil war history in our family. My great-grandparents (my mother's grandparents) were alive when I was a child, and I remember walking down the road to their house and eating tea cakes that my great-grandma made. My great-grandparents were born during a time when being a Negro was extremely difficult. They were supposed to be free, but their struggle to become full citizens with access to the American Dream wasn't available to them. They had no resources: no shelter, no food, no clothing, no job, and no education. They had to do what most other freed Negroes had to do after slavery during the Jim Crow era – go and work the fields for people whose families were likely former slave owners, so they could eat, live and raise their family.

I am the descendent of former slaves and share-croppers. They couldn't read or write. They only had their hands to use to survive. Somehow they survived and had a beautiful family, as they struggled to put food on the table each day and lived in shelter similar to a third world country.

It seems that my ancestors had nothing of value to pass on to their children. No legacy. I was often so taken by the history that one of my co-workers who would share with me about her Greek ancestry, homeland, relatives and travel abroad to reunite with her family. Wow, what a legacy to have in this life! It must be wonderful to know who you are and where you come from and to know your family history. What I would give to be able to have such a legacy for my children and me. I feel like an orphan, disconnected from my line of ancestors for so many generations with the knowledge of my family history only beginning with the end of the Civil War.

Well, another one of those lemons in my life. But, once again, God revealed a sweet blessing to me that once again turned one of my life's lemons into lemonade. This was literally a truly sweet memory. As I searched for a connection to my past, I discovered that I indeed had a legacy that was passed on by generations that could neither read nor write. These sweet memories were the recipes shared by my grandmas and passed on to me over the years that I use frequently as I prepare meals for my family.

I have a legacy of sweet memories that I want to share with you that make up my journey in life. These sweet memories provided me with moments during my childhood that give me a legacy to pass on to the next generation. I am forever thankful to my wonderful grandmas who created such sweet memories for me in my life, when they probably had difficulties of their own that I did not even know about. These were fun times in my life and over the past 25 years I have tried to research and preserve these special recipes that offered delicious memories during my childhood.

Our family has a legacy of recipes that have been passed on from prior generations – our sweet memories. I was blessed to have many wonderful people in my life and appreciate the sweet memories that they created to provide me with this sweet legacy that they offered to me during my childhood. I didn't have the riches that the world had to offer, that other children may have had, I wasn't born into the race that had access to all that America and the world had to offer, I was born into a life destined for exclusion and struggles. I was born in a barrel filled with lemons.

But, I discovered that God was with me, regardless of my status in life. I knew that he didn't love me any less than he loved those who were born to have access to every advantage in life for many generations. I knew that the Scriptures say that I am special to God, and once again, God showed me how to make lemonade out of life's lemons. He gave me sweet memories of family recipes, created by great cooks in my grandmas' kitchens. I have a special gift that I can pass on to the next generation – a legacy of sweet memories.

I would like to share some of my sweet memories with you. Maybe by sharing my sweet memories, it will help you discover how to turn lemons in your life into sweet lemonade.

The Tea Cake

The tea cake recipe is one of the oldest family recipes and is believed to have originated during slavery. This recipe is special because my family lost it, because it was not made by many in the post-slavery generations. My great-grandparents were the last generation that made those special "tea cakes" in my family. No one in my family makes tea cakes today. I believe that one surviving family member in my husband's family still makes them.

The tea cake looks like a brown cookie in my family, but a white biscuit in my husband's family. It depends on your family's heritage and ancestry. When my husband and I talked about the wonderful taste of the tea cake, we thought that we were remembering the same treat. But, we discovered that our memories and our tea cakes were different. Apparently, our families had many similar experiences, but some of our recipes are prepared differently. We never knew that we had different tea cakes as children until after I had finished my 25 years of research and experiments to re-create my lost family recipe.

I had not had a tea cake since I was a child. I was very young when I had my last one. As I remember the last time I had a tea cake as a child. I could smell the sweet, unique aroma flowing outside the screened door, finding its way to my nose, as I played outside. Oh my, what is that wonderful smell? It seemed to be calling me, taking over all my senses. My mouth began to fill with water as my taste buds became activated by that sweet, sweet smell. I stopped playing and walked toward that sweet smell, through the door into the kitchen. Then, I looked up and a sweet brown delight was placed into my little hand. I took a bite and the treat just melted in my mouth. That heavenly smell and delightful taste still remains vividly within my mind even today.

Whatever happened to that treat? I decided to contact my mom about the tea cake recipe. "Hey mom, do you have the tea cake recipe from those special treats that we had a long time ago?" "No. I don't have the recipe," she replied. "The last generation that made the tea cake in our family was your great-grandmother who passed away when you were a child." I asked, "Do you remember how to make the tea cake?" She answered, "No."

I was disappointed. Who else may remember how to make the tea cake in my family? Surely, Grandma Eddie Mae, who is always cooking, would remember the tea cake recipe. I called Grandma Eddie Mae. "Good afternoon, Grandma, it's Gail. I was wondering if you remember the tea cake recipe." "Goodness no," responded Grandma, "I don't remember anyone making the tea cakes in my generation. Tea cakes haven't been made for decades, and I don't know anyone who would know how to make them today. I haven't had a tea cake since I was a child. That is a very old recipe and people didn't write back then, so that recipe is probably lost forever."

I asked each one of my grandmas, but none of them remembered the recipe made so long ago. I asked everyone in my family whom I could think of that may have any information regarding that old family recipe, but the answer was always the same – "NO recipe."

I became determined to restore that lost family recipe. After no one in my family had any records or memory of how to make the tea cakes, I decided to look outside of my family.

Maybe my husband's family also enjoyed the tea cake. My husband remembered the tea cake too and thought that maybe someone in his family may still have the recipe. I called my mother-in-law for her family's recipe. She has shared wonderful recipes with me in the past, and I knew that she would share the tea cake recipe with me, if she had it. But, the phone call ended the same way as the call ended with my family. No, she didn't have the recipe for the tea cake. It was made by the previous generation, so she couldn't provide me with any information.

That was over 25 years ago. I decided that the tea cake recipe was too important to be lost, so I starting constantly asking relatives to try to remember the ingredients, try to recall the memories, all in an attempt to reconstruct this lost recipe. Over the years, I would receive an occasional call and get an ingredient that someone would remember. Others would describe the taste to me, while others described the smell. But, they all knew exactly what special smell and taste I was trying to recover.

Then, my mom called one evening and said that she had a dream and remembered the ingredients in the tea cake recipe. She said that she had a dream and could clearly see her grandmother (my great-grandmother) making those special treats. That same weekend, my sister-in-law, Cheryl, called and she also had information on the ingredients to the tea cake recipe. That was wonderful. It seemed that I had enough information to start experimenting with the combination of ingredients.

As a result of my persistence, to re-construct my family's lost family tea cake recipe, I discovered that the tea cake recipe of my husband's family and my family were different. My husband's family's tea cake was white and looked like a biscuit and had a lemon favor. While my family's tea cake recipe was brown and sweeter and tasted more like a cookie.

Well, the experiments to perfect those little treats would not happen overnight. It would take months of trying various combinations of ingredients, just to achieve a result that at least looked like the tea cake. I was disappointed when the tea cakes looked exactly as I remembered, but didn't smell or taste as I remembered. Once again, I had to call relatives and ask them to call other relatives to try to figure out what was still missing.

It took much longer to perfect both recipes to get the treats to taste and smell like the tea cakes that my husband and I remembered. My husband wanted to have a taste of his past, after I accidentally discovered his lost childhood tea cake treat, while searching for my lost childhood tea cake treat.

Finally, I modified the combinations of ingredients, by reflecting back on what was available for cooking ingredients in that time period that are not consistent with the ingredients I was using from this time period.

I think I know the answer. Let me give my mom and sister-in-law one last call, now that I was reconstructing two recipes instead of one recipe. After another conversation with both my mom and my sister-in-law, I modified both recipes and made both to see if I had finally rediscovered the lost treats from our past. Oh my – that smell – I remember that sweet smell that filled the kitchen as those treats baked in the oven. Now, it is time for the final test – the taste – oh my! This tastes like my lost treat! Then, my husband smiled with delight – this tastes like my lost treat, too!

Oh what a wonderful evening we had enjoying our special treats that were 25 years in the making.

My Family's Tea Cake Recipe (Malone Family)

The following tea cakes recipe from my family is based upon verbal interviews with my mother, Juanita (Murray) Mosley, who recalled the recipe made by Mama Sue Malone, her grandmother and my great-grandmother. The original tea cakes recipes were made for large quantities to serve a large family. The quantities reflected in the recipe below were reduced to reflect today's portion size.

Ingredients:
- 1 cup plain flour
- 1 teaspoon baking powder
- Salt (dash)
- ½ teaspoon nutmeg (fresh nutmeg is best)
- 4 tablespoons butter
- ¾ cup sugar
- ½ teaspoon vanilla
- 1 egg
- 2 tablespoons molasses

Directions:

Shift together (*keep in separate bowl*) – flour, baking powder, salt, and nutmeg (*this is your flour mixture*)

Mix other ingredients and cream – butter, sugar, vanilla flavor, egg, and molasses

Use a separate container and pour in a portion of the creamed mixture. Gradually add the flour mixture and stir. Continue to add and mix the flour mixture until you have a "biscuit or pie crust" texture and consistency. Sprinkle a little flour mixture on a pastry board (or use waxed paper, foil or cutting board if you don't have a pastry board) until you have a biscuit/pie crust-type dough that you can hold in your hand without the dough sticking to your fingers. Roll out the dough and use a small glass or cup to cut out small cookies. Place the cut cookie dough onto a cookie sheet (sprayed with a cooking spray) and bake at 350° until the bottom of the cookies is slightly brown and crusted. Watch the cookies carefully, because the baking time is relatively short.

My Husband's Family's Tea Cake Recipe (Parrish Family)

While researching my family's tea cakes recipe my husband and I discovered that our childhood treats were different. We were not talking about the same tea cake. The following tea cakes recipe was provided to me by my sister-in-law Cheryl (Conner) Broughton, after making numerous contacts to her about the ingredients of the long-lost tea cakes recipe. The quantities reflected in the recipe below were also reduced to reflect today's portion size.

Ingredients:
- 1 cup plain flour
- 1 teaspoon baking powder
- ½ teaspoon nutmeg
- 2 tablespoons butter
- ½ cup sugar
- ½ teaspoon vanilla flavor
- ½ teaspoon lemon flavor
- 1 egg

Note: As a result of researching the Parrish family tea cakes recipe, two variations were discovered. One version of the recipe includes the ingredient nutmeg, while excluding buttermilk (the one above). The other version excludes nutmeg, but includes buttermilk (my husband's Aunt Leona Aston's recipe). Thus, the Parrish family recipe has two optional ingredients – nutmeg and buttermilk, depending on your taste preference.

You may want to experiment with these two variations of this delicious family recipe to discover which taste you prefer.

Directions:

Shift together (keep in separate bowl) – flour, baking powder, and nutmeg (*this is your flour mixture*)

Mix other ingredients and cream – butter, sugar, vanilla flavor, lemon favor, and egg.

Use a separate container and pour in a portion of the creamed mixture. Gradually add the flour mixture and stir. Continue to add and mix the flour mixture until you have a "biscuit or pie crust" texture and consistency. Sprinkle a little flour mixture on a pastry board (or use waxed paper, foil or cutting board if you don't have a pastry board) until you have a biscuit/pie crust-type dough that you can hold in your hand without the dough sticking to your fingers. ,Roll out the dough and use a small glass or cup to cut out small cookies. Place the cut cookie dough onto a cookie sheet (sprayed with a cooking spray) and bake at 350° until the bottom of the cookies is slightly brown and crusted. Watch the cookies carefully, because the baking time is relatively short.

Grandma Willie Mae's Sweet Legacy of Memories

I spent part of the summer in Mississippi with my other grandma, which was also a treat. She was a wonderful cook and I especially loved her homemade praline candies and chicken and dumplings. When I arrived at my grandma's I requested my two homemade favorites. She loved to cook. She went outside, picked up a chicken from the yard and proceeded to ring its neck. She placed the chicken in a black boiling pot of water and told me to pick the feathers off of the chicken to get it prepared for dinner. She had a beautiful garden full of fresh vegetables next to her house. Even her flowerbeds were filled with vegetables, including tomatoes, hot peppers, bell peppers, squash, and collard greens. We gathered vegetables from the flowerbeds and garden and prepared a delicious meal that included hot corn bread (that was distinctly sweet, and sometimes she would add hot crackling to the corn bread to make it spicy), collard greens, and chicken and dumpling.

I loved to watch her make the dough for the dumplings – rolling, cutting and folding nice plump pieces of the uncooked dough and throwing it into the pot of boiling seasoned broth and chicken. She added lots of spices and the smell filled the house. After we finished eating my special meal, Grandma began to search for a pot that she could use to make her homemade praline candy. She explained how to make the candy and that it had to get to the "soft ball" stage. She didn't have a candy thermometer. Instead, she used a bowl with a dish of cold water to test the candy to determine if it was at the right temperature. She dropped a small amount of the candy into the water and watched for the perfect response that indicated that the candy was ready for the next phase or needed to cook longer. I have included this special southern sweet memory recipe in this book for you.

Grandma Willie Mae's Homemade Sweet Southern Praline Candy Recipe
(Gail's Mississippi childhood memory)

Ingredients:
3 cups brown sugar
¼ teaspoon salt
1 cup cream or milk *(heavy cream is my preference)*
1 to 2 tablespoons of butter
1 teaspoon vanilla
1 cup of pecans

Directions: *(a candy thermometer is recommended, unless you know how to use the cold water in the bowl method)*

Combine –
3 cups brown sugar
¼ teaspoon salt
1 cup cream or milk

Cover and cook about 3 minutes until steam has washed down crystals from side of pot.

Uncover and cook slowly without stirring to a soft ball stage (238 degrees Fahrenheit). Remove candy from heat and add: 1 to 2 tablespoons of butter. Cool to 110 degrees Fahrenheit. Beat until smooth and creamy. Add 1 teaspoon vanilla and pecans. Drop candy from spoon (and shape) onto buttered surface (or spray with a non-stick cooking spray). *Enjoy!*

Note: My Grandma never wrote down the above recipe. I would watch Grandma during my visits home over 25 years ago and document the procedure. Later, I would practice until I got the recipe right (sometimes after a call to Grandma to discuss my initial problems with duplicating her candy-making technique).

Note: I only use fresh pecans, typically ordered from Georgia, Mississippi or from my family homestead in Alabama where pecan trees are in our front yard. Unfortunately, most of the pecan trees were destroyed by hurricanes over the past years with the greatest devastation by Hurricane Katrina. Pecans in packages at the store may not work well if they are soft. Sometimes, good, firm southern pecans are available during the Thanksgiving and Christmas holidays after the fall harvest. Store candy after cooled in a sealed airtight container.

Grandma Eddie Mae's Legacy of Memories

I spent many days and nights with different relatives. I was especially fond of staying at my Grandma Eddie Mae's house (actually my great-aunt and my Grandma Viola's sister). Grandma Eddie Mae was the wife of my Uncle Preston (my great uncle – I don't know why I called him Uncle Preston and his wife Grandma – *who can figure out why children do things anyway*?). They were both devoted God-fearing Christians, and Uncle Preston was a deacon in our church. It was with Grandma Eddie Mae and Uncle Preston that I learned how to churn butter, harvest eggs, and set the table for Sunday dinner to entertain guests. These were special times when the minister, deacons and friends would come over for a grand afternoon of great food (especially her home-made biscuits – *a recipe I am still trying to master* – and banana pudding served with wonderful percolating coffee that filled the house with an unbelievable aroma.

Grandma Eddie Mae had two sons, but no girls. She had arthritis, so I would go over on weekends and after school to help with ironing, churning butter, or anything else that she wanted me to do. She would always bake me a tiny little cake in a small little black skillet. It was just for me, whenever she made a cake for the family or for guests. How I loved my special little treat that was just for me! It was a little piece of heaven on earth. I seemed to have no concerns in life while at Grandma Eddie Mae's house.

Sometimes, she would let me help her cook. She even trusted me to prepare one of the dishes for the minister and deacons who would be coming to her home after church one Sunday. Grandma Eddie Mae always entertained the ministers and prepared grand meals for them to enjoy after church on Sundays and on other occasions.

I was very excited. I would prepare a dish. Now what would I prepare? I know, the potato salad would be my special dish. I cut up the potatoes, mixed all the ingredients into a pretty flowered bowl, and placed the completed dish in the refrigerator until it was time to serve the meal. The guests arrived. People chatted for a while as the women were preparing the table. Grandma was busy getting everything on the table, and then she reminded me to get my potato salad and place it on the table. I ran to the kitchen and quickly removed my special dish from the refrigerator and placed it on the table. It looked beautiful. I was proud of the dish that I had prepared. Everything was perfect.

Uncle Preston blessed the food. The different dishes were passed around the table for the guests to put a portion on their plates. Then, the minister placed a portion of the potato salad on his plate. I looked with excitement, because the minister was going to eat a dish that I had prepared. He placed his fork into the potato salad and the fork went into his mouth. The look on his face was confusing – what's wrong? Did I forget the salt? He looked and then reached for a napkin to remove the potato salad from his mouth. He looked at my Grandma and said – I think that someone forgot to cook the potatoes. Oh no, what a nightmare. What embarrassment. In all my excitement and trying to remember all the ingredients, I had forgotten the most important step – I forgot to cook the potatoes! There was laughter and apologies to the guests. My Grandma Eddie Mae looked over at me and we both got up from the table as she removed the dish. But, she never said that I had prepared the potato salad. She never said anything in front of the guests.

As we walked to the kitchen quietly, she whispered to me, "I can't believe that you forgot to cook the potatoes before making the potato salad. Well, the next time I bet you will remember to cook those potatoes." That was my first attempt at cooking and entertaining guests independent of the oversight of Grandma. But, not a discouraging word came out of her mouth. Of course, her two sons laughed and teased me after the guests left, because they knew who had prepared that dish of uncooked potato salad. But, they too didn't choose to say anything in front of the guests. Everyone just laughed and continued with the rest of the meal.

Now, I consider myself an excellent cook even though my start was somewhat less than perfect.

Wonderful memories were created in my second home at Grandma's.

Don't Forget Dad

My mom is an excellent cook too! Her sweet potato pie, pecan pie, fruit cake, blackberry cobbler and pecan cake are my favorites. Her desserts are unique and recipes are quite difficult to master. But, just for the record, women are not the only good cooks in our family. My dad is a great cook, too. But, not the sweet stuff. His specialty includes southern seafood gumbo and barbecue ribs. But, dad has kept his recipes a secret including his barbecue sauce recipe. He jokingly assures me that he will share his recipes with me before he dies. Until he decides to share his secrets, we will just have to enjoy his special meals. My daughter, Courtney, prefers her grandpa's ribs and gumbo to mine. She waits on her grandpa to ship his ribs to her wherever she is living or for him to make her gumbo when he visits us on the East Coast. She will call him and put in her cooking requests, and of course, she gets what she wants from him without hesitation.

Once, I took my ribs and my dad's ribs to church for fellow church members to determine whose ribs were the best. I was over the Vacation Bible School program for the year and I included an adult evening program that was called The Venus Tea Room. We would have special events each evening for the adults, while the children participated in the Vacation Bible School program. Each evening, I would bring in special foods, usually ordered from local restaurants. But, one evening, I decided to include barbecue ribs on the menu. This would be a good opportunity to have an unbiased comparison of my ribs and my dad's ribs, and find out whose ribs are the best. But, I lost that competition. It seemed that most people selected my dad's ribs as the best ribs. Of course, my husband, Curtis, thought that my ribs were the best!

My dad doesn't write down his recipes. But, that's OK. I have been watching him and documenting what he does, and eventually, I plan on duplicating his specialties. But today, I am still a student of the trade, not the master that he has become. I will keep watching, documenting and experimenting until I master his techniques.

Over the years, I have often baked sweet treats for my family. I make Curtis' favorite desserts such as homemade German chocolate cake, carrot cake, or Boston Cream cheesecake (southern style with pecans). I enjoy taking the warm chocolate chip cookies or cream cheese brownies out of the oven, putting them on small plates, and taking them while they are still hot, to my children's rooms, where they are usually playing video games, studying or watching a movie. As they have gone off to college, I prepare their special sweet treats and other favorite dishes and take them to them during my visits.

I have chosen to pass on to my family the Legacy of Sweet Memories!

CHAPTER 10

The Wisdom of Children

My journey that started so long ago in 1968 had ended with the trip to Africa in 2006. An amazing transformation had happened to me over those years and to our nation. I no longer had the lemons (life changing moments) in my life. I had stopped making lemonade to survive life's unpleasant challenges in my life. Lemons were gradually disappearing, as I grew older. I had transformed along with society and that transformation resulted in my dealing with the challenges in life in a completely different way.

The Wisdom of Children

After we moved to the North East, our search for a church initially resulted in our following the old habit of looking for an all-black Baptist church that was similar to our former churches in Alabama. We were looking to raise our children in the same type of religious environment that we were raised in. However, during our search, we discovered that the style of worship in the black churches that we visited was different from what we remembered. The worship services in the southern black Baptist churches in Alabama were different.

We eventually joined a black church in Pennsylvania in the community where my husband worked at the time. The music was exceptional in that church. My home church choir in Alabama didn't have a lot of talented singers, but the members of the choir sang to the glory of God to the best of their abilities. However, the church that my husband grew up in had great choirs and a seemingly endless supply of extremely gifted singers and musicians. The music at his church was awesome! The people were nice at the church that we had joined in Pennsylvania, and the worship service was nice, but I felt out of place – something was wrong – not with the church, but with me. But, my husband seemed happy with our new church, so I didn't say anything about how I was feeling. Maybe I would get used to this new part of the country and this different style of worship.

One morning, as we were driving to church with our three children buckled into their car and booster seats, my oldest son blurted out an unexpected statement that changed the course of our family and our focus as parents. We were listening to gospel music as we drove toward our final destination for Sunday worship. Curtis was singing along with the music. The children and I just sat quietly as he drove us to church that morning. We left early that Sunday morning, because we wanted to get to the church in time for Sunday school.

Our son spoke with a loud voice. The voice of a child re-directed the path of our family. The voice of a young child was used to put our entire family on the road that God intended for us to travel. If that child had not spoken and worst, if we as parents had not listened, I would have never made the journey home to Africa. I would have never received my special gift that God had prepared for me. I would have never finished my journey. I guess you are wondering what a small child could ever say to parents that would get their attention with a message so strong that it would change their path, the path of their children, and the path of their family.

Our son Brian said, "I hate this church". I don't think he meant hate in the true sense, but it was the only way a four-year-old could say what he meant. God did use him to get our attention. My husband and I looked at each other, concerned by the comments of our child. I felt that I had failed as a parent, not because of his statement, but because I had failed to put the Christian education of my children ahead of what type of church service gave me pleasure and was comfortable for me to attend.

My parents, Uncle Preston, my Sunday school teachers, and even my third grade teacher in the Negro-only public elementary school had all contributed to my Christian education. They had all made my Christian education a priority. Without that Christian educational foundation, I would not have the personal relationship with God (salvation from that sermon when I was a child that gave me the message of "Don't follow the crowd," so I could overcome my trials, my struggles, my tribulations, and my lemons. I would not have the knowledge (God's words – the Bible, the memory of the 23rd Psalm) that would provide me with one of the tools that I needed to handle the childhood crises (lemons) in my life.

I realized that I had failed to provide my children with the Christian education that they needed. I had failed as a mother to search for the place that God intended for them, not me, so they could be taught by the Christian community – the Christian village that would meet their needs. I realized my time was passing, and my journey was ending, but my children's journey had already begun and they had not been adequately prepared. My children lacked the foundation that had been given to me. They lacked the armor of God. I was so focused on my own needs and personal struggles that I didn't realize that I was failing my children.

Parents are not capable of providing for all the needs of children to create the stable foundation that they need to deal with life's challenges (their lemons in life). My children, just like me, needed the Christian community to help them travel life's journey for their lives. Parents, who try to be everything for their children may leave big gaps in their lives, gaps that can't be filled by us parents, gaps that will be filled by others. It is up to the parents to choose who will fill those gaps – their peers, friends, television, movies, Internet, social clubs, or some unknown stranger who steals your place in their lives. I had a choice as a parent, and I chose to look for the place of worship that would provide my children with the Christian community that God had planned for them.

After my son's statement, my husband and I looked at each other and laughed out loud. We both understood the message, because we were both privately experiencing the same type of discomfort that our children must have been experiencing. The church was wonderful. It just wasn't the path that God intended for my children or our family to travel. No, God was preparing our family for a different purpose in life, a different path.

In Psalm 139, verses 13 and 14 say *"For you created my inmost being; you knit me together in my mother's womb. I praise you because I am fearfully and wonderfully made; your works are wonderful, I know that full well."*

As I looked at my beautiful three children all buckled in comfortably in the back of our minivan, I reflected on that verses in Psalm 139 and I knew what I had to do for my children. We were a long way from our hometown in Alabama where family and others in the Christian community could be so involved in our lives that they felt free to reprimand our inappropriate conduct and communicate our behavior to our parents when we were children. We had moved to a place where we had no family, no relationships, no community, no grandparents and no great-grandparents to support the nurturing of our children.

We were alone as a family with shelter, food, clothing, and careers, and we thought that we were successfully providing for our family. We had tried to find a church home and become a part of the community, but we were foreigners to this local church membership. We were not a part of their community as children so they didn't know us, they didn't know our family, and they didn't know our children. We were alone in that large congregation on Sunday mornings, surrounded by people who looked like us. We were indeed strangers, not a part of the Christian community.

On that Sunday morning, the void and disconnect in the lives of our children was exposed vividly – seemingly to both my husband and me instantly, because it seemed to free us. We both knew that we were on the wrong path for our children's foundation in life. They needed more than nice clothes, trips to Chucky Cheese and walks in the park. They needed a Christian community that would meet their needs where they could grow up and travel the journey that God intended for them.

We had offered to them what we thought as parents was best for them based upon what we thought they needed – to grow up in a black church, so they could have some form of identity. But, we were on the wrong path. The identity we were trying to provide for them wasn't even our true identity. It was a fragmented substitute for the identity that had been taken from us, because of the race we were born into on earth.

The black church was not a place to pass on to our children their culture or identity, it was a place of emotional revival and a place where the wounds of life could be bandaged up on Sundays, so that the wounded Christian soldiers could get treatment and return to the battlefield of life on Monday morning. It was a place of refuge and strength where the intensity of the music and songs provided the emotional healing experiences, and the words of the minister provided words of encouragement and hope to the congregation, so they could survive the battles in their lives.

That church met the needs of that community. My husband and I benefited from the black church experience, but our children's needs were different and their needs were not being met. So, I understood what my son meant by his statement that he hated that church experience, because he could not relate to the intensity of the services. It was too much for him, and to be honest, sometimes it was too much for me as well. Sometimes, I could feel the pain overflowing into the audience during the services. That place had been prepared by God to meet the needs of the people in that community, but my needs and my children's needs were different at that time in our lives. Clearly, we were in the wrong place of worship. Our family's life was headed for change and new experiences that I didn't even know existed. Once again, I would discover another world in our society that created advantages for those who had the knowledge, access and resources to gain the benefit that would provide opportunities and some educational luxuries that I never even knew existed. We would eventually discover that was not the only wrong path that we had taken before finding the right road of life for our children to begin their travels.

That Sunday morning, after the bold statement by our son, my husband turned the minivan around before we arrived at the church and we returned home. We didn't talk about that Sunday morning experience that day. But, the following Sunday morning, my husband got up as usual to get prepared for Sunday worship and shocked me with his words, "What is it with this family? I live with some apparently strong family members." My husband looked at me and said that he was going to visit a new church today. Apparently, he had started searching for a new place of worship for our family, so we never returned to the other church that my son had made the bold statement about. My husband would come home Sunday after Sunday after his visits to different churches in the area. We would go with him to a church that he had identified as a possibility, but we couldn't find a place that felt right for our family. How can there be so many churches, but we couldn't find one place that we felt was the right fit for our family?

My husband finally found this non-denominational church that he thought was a possibility. They met in a rented school building and had a mixed congregation. We had grown tired of searching and were getting frustrated with our inability to find the right place for our family. This church was very different from what I was familiar with. It was an evangelical charismatic-type church and the church had a praise group that included instruments, such as drums. I had grown-up with the piano and organ, I was not familiar with this type of worship format, and I didn't recognize any of the music.

Because of my husband's music background and singing in the college choir that traveled across the country, he easily adapted to the new music and style of worship and really seemed to enjoy that church. But, I felt uncomfortable; especially with the women 50s type "Leave It to Beaver" roles. I felt like I was in a time warp or something. I also discovered that most of the children were "homeschooled" and didn't interact with many children outside of their church. This was definitely not for me. I had a biology/education degree, but I didn't feel competent enough to teach my children their entire curriculum at home without the interaction of other children and removing the element of competition.

Education to me was more than books. It included exposing your children to an environment that developed their social skills and provided opportunities for competitive sports. An education included developing the body, soul and mind without crushing the spirit of the child. I didn't consider myself capable of providing all those things to my children as their sole educator. I had already realized that I had failed at providing them the Christian education and community that they needed by trying to meet all their needs without the help of others, except for my husband. The occasional visits to their grandparents in the south provided too little exposure for them to gain the benefits that I had gained during my childhood.

But, I am not here to judge those parents who made that choice for their children. I didn't know the needs of their family and children any more than they knew the needs of my family and children. We were still strangers at that church. But, something didn't feel right to me. My husband was really enjoying his church experience, but I didn't feel comfortable with some of the teachings. They seemed to have somewhat of a female gender oppressive environment. I found that the sermons created contradictions in the Scriptures and my Christian educational foundation that I had relied upon for my life.

I was hesitant to say anything to my husband, because I didn't want to spoil things for him since he seemed happy and comfortable with our new place of worship. But, I was very uncomfortable. So, finally I told my husband that I didn't feel comfortable with the church we were attending. I just didn't feel right and I couldn't connect with the sermons, music and anything else at that church. We talked about it, but decided that the church seemed to have a good children's program, so even though I didn't feel comfortable, at least it seemed like a good place for the children. Still, I had concerns and I was not comfortable – not even with the education of my children, because if the sermons caused me anxiety, what if my children were being taught something that was inconsistent with my values and Christian beliefs. I didn't know what to do.

We continued to attend that church, and my feelings never changed. One Sunday after service, as we picked up our children from their Sunday school, one of the men in the church approached my husband and me. He said that he wanted to apologize to us for something that his son had said to my oldest son. He said that he was deeply sorry, and he wanted to apologize, because his son had called our son a Nigger in Sunday school that morning. He assured us that he had no idea where his son had heard that horrible word, and he said that he and his family didn't use that type of language in their home. I was speechless. I was shocked. But, I forgave him and his son, because he asked for our forgiveness.

Wait a minute – it's the 90s now. Surely, I no longer have to worry about a member of my family being called a Nigger. I thought that that era had ended and my children would be spared that pain that I had experienced in 1968 when I attended desegregated schools for the first time. This time, the hate speech was spoken in the place where we were supposed to be safe – church. I had caused my children harm, because I had exposed them to a church that was not all black. So, it provided the opportunity for a white child to hurt my child and my family in the only place I could turn to in life for safety.

This place was not like the place in Wisconsin that was free of racial hatred. This place had racial baggage, and as such, I would never return or allow my children to return again. My husband was free to go if he chose to, but I didn't want my children exposed to hate speech in a place where they needed to develop a personal relationship with God. We seemed to have gone from bad to worse in identifying a Christian community that would provide a healthy environment for our children to be educated and nurtured.

I didn't feel like Pennsylvania would ever become home for me. I longed for the days that I had in Wisconsin. My life and the country were evolving and becoming a better place for all people, but there was no guarantee that you and your children would not be hurt by those who still lived in the past of racial hatred. What would we do now? At that moment, I gave up on finding a church home and community for our family. I no longer enjoyed church. Curtis would always find a church to visit on Sundays, but I started opting out of taking the journey with him. I had given up. It was hard to find a place to fit in. At least, that was how it seemed to me.

Education of Our Children – An Unexpected Change in the Path of Our Family

My children were growing up and it was time for our daughter to go to school. She was ready to begin kindergarten. Each of our children had attended daycare at some point in their lives. We wanted them to learn a foreign language, so we always sought out pre-school locations that taught foreign languages (French and/or Spanish). Having the ability to speak two languages was very important to us, because we wanted our children to master the English language and be proficient in at least one foreign language. We discovered that learning a foreign language in high school is too late. Children need exposure from birth. So, that was an educational priority for us.

I had attended public schools and graduated from a public university. My husband was the product of a public education, too. We never thought about anything else for our children. It had been good enough for us, and it would be good enough for our children. So, my daughter started a kindergarten program in the local public school district. I was very nervous about my first child leaving for school and catching the yellow school bus, but I knew that I'd better not show my anxiety, so that my daughter would not get nervous or afraid. She was a fun-loving and independent-spirited child and a joy as a child. So, I was confident that she would do well and was ready for the change that was coming in her life.

She caught that yellow school bus that day. I waved at her as the bus slowly drove to the next bus stop. I packed my other two children in their car seats in the back of my car and I followed the bus from a distance, so I could make sure that she made it to her destination safely at the local public elementary school. I had prayed that everything would go well for my daughter that first day of school. As her brothers played at home, I waited anxiously for her return. I got out the double stroller and pushed my two sons, as I walked to the bus stop to wait for my daughter to return after her first day had ended.

Things seemed to be going fine, at least on the surface. I got involved in the school where my daughter attended. I frequently spoke with the wonderful principal who made me feel like my child was in the perfect place. I was asked to serve on the School Board's Kindergarten Committee. I thought that I was being a good parent and that my child was in a safe environment for learning. But, I would soon discover that, once again, I had made a mistake in the education of my children. What I envisioned as my child's experience was not the experience of my child. The kindness of the administration and especially the principal provided an unusual feeling of safety for your child. My child finished kindergarten and entered the first grade. We had made friends in the neighborhood and our children had playmates. My husband worked at his professional job and I ran my consulting business, working out of my home, so I could be with my children.

My husband and I both went with our daughter to meet her new teacher. The teacher didn't smile or give eye contact and was not friendly. I was somewhat nervous, but I had no real basis for concern. Maybe she had a bad night and was just tired. So, I smiled and offered to volunteer or help in any way that could support her. But, she didn't even respond to me – it was as though I was not in the room. My husband Curtis asked the teacher about lunch and she said "they're doing something different this year, it's not my concern." He responded and said that "he felt that at this age lunch as well as academics should be your concern." But, she just continued to set up the classroom.

A few weeks later, I was in the local mall with my children. They had an inside play area, so I would take them there to play inside during the day and to participate in the mall children's club activities that was available at the time. This one day, a former neighbor called my name and approached me. She was a young white female who had a child a little older than our daughter, who was attending the same school. We were just talking and catching up on things, when she asked with a smile, "How's your daughter doing in school?" I responded, "OK, I guess." Then she asked who her teacher was? I responded, "Ms. S.," and then she turned as white as a sheet and her faced turned to horror. She said, "Get your child out of that teacher's class. She destroys children. She destroyed our lives. Our son started wetting the bed again, because of the stress inflicted on him in her classroom. I didn't know she taught the grade that your daughter is in. I thought that your child was safe or I would have warned you about her earlier. I am sorry, but please, get your child out of that school and away from that woman. She has tenure so they just seem to move her around as parents find out about her. They pick children to be in her class that are quiet, passive and are not a discipline problem, so that is probably why your child ended up with her. Your daughter is so sweet, quiet and disciplined. She was perfect for that woman's class."

I explained that I was on the Kindergarten Committee and had not heard about any of this before. She said, "Honey – wake up. Do you think that they would tell you something like that? They protect the teachers, not the children. Just don't let her do to your child what she did to my child! Protect your child!"

I was horrified by this news and my heart broke as I thought about the potential pain my child must have experienced. In my heart, I felt that something was wrong and the issue related to the children knowing when it was time to eat lunch caused me concern. But, this was the final straw. Just like my parents had no idea of the experience that I had with the teacher that I had in the sixth grade, I was completely unaware of the experience that my daughter was having. This was unacceptable to me. I became angry at the system that had reversed the priorities that existed when I attended public schools so many years before. What had gone wrong?

I prayed to God for help. What can I do? How can I protect my children from harm? This had nothing to do with race or gender – this was different.

When I got home, I told my husband about the conversation at the mall. I told him that I was going to look for another place for our child's education. I didn't know where she would go, but I had to find her a place where she would be cared about in an educational environment that could be trusted.

The next morning, I sent my daughter off to school. My husband decided to try to talk to the teacher, but afterward, he knew, too, that we had to find another place for our child.

I began my search for a private school. We couldn't afford it, but somehow God would have to provide lemonade again, because our daughter had a lemon for a teacher and an administration and system that protected the teacher, not our child. I pulled out the yellow pages and started calling every school in the area. I would drive around communities and look for private schools in the area. Wow, this is not easy and I was very worried about the expense of a private school education. But, I was willing to work two or three jobs to do what I had to do to pay for my child's safety.

I finally found the perfect place for our child. It was a private Lutheran church school. I spoke to someone on the phone and they were very nice. I scheduled a visit and met the teachers and administrator. It was a small school that only went to the sixth grade. The transition from public education to private education was never even a consideration for me as a parent. But, here we were, out of necessity, forced to look for other educational options.

There were no black teachers at that school, but there was the type of love, acceptance and colorless inclusion that I had experienced so long before in Wisconsin at the church that we had integrated. My husband and I were very active at this new school that our daughter attended.

It was perfect!

It turned out to be a double blessing for our family. I was talking to someone at Christ Memorial Lutheran School one day and mentioned that we were looking for a church. She smiled and then said, "There is a church only a few miles away where y'all folks attend." I didn't know what to make of the statement. She said that they would love to have us join their Lutheran church family, but she knew that there was a better place for us. She then said, "Why don't you try and visit those *folks* at Paoli Baptist. I think that you will be happy with what you find."

I told my husband about the comment and he decided to check it out. It was on the Main Line, an affluent part of the suburban community, located on the main street that connects the suburbs with the city of Philadelphia. I said to my husband, "What a strange place to have a black church in this area, but go and see what the service is like." We still had not found a church home – that community that we were looking for to be a part of, so we could raise our family in a socially healthy environment. We had finally found the right place to educate our child. But, we still had not found a place to provide our children with a Christian education that only comes by being a part of a local church that becomes your home, your community, and your family.

Curtis visited that church where we were told that *"y'all folks"* attended. We both had assumed that the person was referring to an all-black church. But, Curtis told me that when he drove into the church parking lot, he expected to find a group of snobs inside. But, we soon discovered that the southern *"y'all* reference made had nothing to do with the race of the people attending that church. We were shocked to find a diverse congregation made up of a large number of people from the south.

Wow! What a perfect gift. We had finally found our Christian community, because God had brought us to the place where we would worship even to this day and raise our children. We found our community. I am finally able to make Pennsylvania my home. Our relationships and community over the years would be beyond the walls of that church, beyond one race of people, and even beyond exposure to one type of religion. We joined that Southern Baptist Church so many years ago and our children received a wonderful Christian educational foundation that would shape their futures.

That foundation would cause the path of our daughter to look toward the mission fields, beyond the borders of this country, and choose a path that would take her farther and me on a journey to Africa to the motherland. My journey would cause suppressed memories to surface and wounds to heal. It is unlikely that we would have been prepared to join this type of congregation if we had not had that positive experience in Wisconsin so many years before in that white congregation that we joined. Joining this church involved no stress, no lemons and no lemonade. We had finally identified the educational paths for our children – academic and religious. All my children accepted Christ as their personal Savior and were all baptized at this church. My husband became a deacon. I became a Sunday school teacher. Eventually, my husband would become the worship leader, too.

Our children would never return to the public education system. Our children would move from the Christian Lutheran school to the Quaker school where I would begin my Valentine's Balls for them and their classmates. My husband and I have always made it a top priority to be very active in the schools that educate our children, with my husband serving on the boards of two of the schools they attended. I always worked to support and serve the teachers that I entrusted my children to, serving them in every way possible. I was the homeroom mom most of their elementary years. I wanted to support the teachers as much as possible.

There was one special teacher in the lives of our children at the Media-Providence Friends school, Teacher Shirley. She was the world's best teacher. She had a special gift that met the needs of our children in such a special way. I appreciate all those wonderful teachers who educated our child and who didn't cause them harm. But, there is a special place in my heart for Teacher Shirley. There was no other teacher whom I have ever encountered as special as she was, and who was loved so much by our two sons. My daughter didn't have the opportunity to have Teacher Shirley as her teacher, but she was perfect for our sons and exactly what they needed at that stage of their young lives.

"Thank you so much, Teacher Shirley, I will always love you. I felt that our children were the safest when they were in your care. I couldn't have made my sons feel more loved even if I were their teacher."

Our Empty Nest

Our nest has grown empty with the years passing so fast. All three of our children are in college this year, with our daughter beginning her first year of graduate school at Johns Hopkins University, to pursue her Masters degree in Public Policy. She has such a heart for helping people. Our oldest son graduates from Virginia Wesleyan College (a Methodist College) this year with a bachelor's degree in Psychology. Our youngest son is in his Sophomore year at Marist College (a Catholic College) pursuing a Communications/Gaming/Interactive Media degree and is a writing minor. It is so wonderful to see a generation, which has our heritage, now being able to pursue dreams.

I didn't think about pursing dreams as a child. I just struggled to survive, evolving into a career as a result of my childhood experiences. If I had been born in a generation that could dream, I would have probably become a veterinarian, because of my love for animals. But, that wasn't an option as an occupation that I was aware of when I was a child. I have no regrets. I wouldn't change anything. I have exhausted my potential in this short lifetime, daring to reach beyond the expectations of others, daring to live life to the fullest. No, I wouldn't change anything. I am glad that I am a risk taker. I am glad that I don't fear change, but embrace change or sometimes even cause change. That is my function in life – to be an agent of change, not intimidated by peer pressure and having the ability to have an independent mind that is not manipulated by the crowd.

Yes, I am glad that I am capable of working on the team, leading a team, or when necessary, walking alone, even when the path is easier if I would follow the crowd and take the popular positions, when I know that that position is wrong or that it will harm those who can't fight for themselves. Yes, God has made me a strong woman with the ability to demonstrate my unbelievable love by giving you my best, but not afraid to stand firm, and feel the strength that comes from God when the time demands that I prepare to fight the battle.

Our nest became empty in 2007. I wondered how I would handle my children being gone. I worried about how their dad would handle them not being with us as they moved into adulthood. Of course I had my pet Beagle (Buttercup) to keep me company. But, I wondered how the quiet emptiness of our home would make me feel. I didn't want the children to worry about me. So, I pushed them out of the nest and watched them spread their wings and fly. That was my job as a mom. I had nurtured and cared for them and had given them my best. My career was secondary to their love and care.

I realized that none of our children was majoring in the field of study that their father and I both pursued. We are both biologists and I had hoped to pass the business on to one of our children. But, I didn't dare tell them about that possibility, because I worried about if I really wanted my children to experience the rejection and struggles that I had experienced as a business owner. I didn't want to pass on a legacy of pain to my children. So, instead of planting the seeds in their minds about being a biologist or a business owner, I desired to help them discover their unique gifts and abilities, so they could become the woman and men God had planned for them to become.

All three of our children are very unique with different talents and interests. So, my job was to help them discover how to get on their special path in life, not to create a burden that they would somehow disappoint me if they didn't become a biologist, a lawyer or an entrepreneur. Each one of our children chose three different career paths and chose colleges in three different states on the East Coast. I am proud of all three of them and of their discipline, personal choices, and performance in college.

As a mother, I had given them my best. Unlike the strict home that I was raised in as a child, I chose to provide my children with a lot of independence. I didn't want to force them to grow up, but rather, to do as I did in elementary school – watch my beautiful flowers grow. While other parents would talk about the difficulty of raising teenagers, I had a different experience with my children, because those were my favorite years, the years we had fun together, the Valentine's Party years. I knew them and I knew their friends, because those events allowed me to have a closer position near the center of their young lives.

I could sense their struggles, share their joys, and this close connection expanded beyond our children to their friends. Teenagers would freely engage me in conversations about their lives and career choices, and ask me for my opinion about what potential I could see in them. Yes, my healing parties had given me much more than I had ever expected, as I reflected back over the years that included so many special moments with so many teenagers. The teenagers always came to our home to visit, so our children rarely went to the homes of their friends.

It seemed that they wanted to come to Mrs. Conner's house. But, I guess those fresh baked cookies that I cooked added to their desire to come to our home. The teens were from different ethnic backgrounds, different religious backgrounds (Christian, Jewish, no-religion), and different economic backgrounds (poor, middle class, wealthy, very wealthy).

Now that my nest was empty, there would be no more parties. No more children in middle and high school. Everyone had gone.

A Son's Challenge

I had given my youngest son a voter registration card, so he could register to vote. My daughter and older son quickly completed my request when they turned 18, and I expected the same from our youngest child. But, weeks had passed and he still had not completed the voter registration card. This is very important and I didn't understand why he had not completed this simple task. It would take about five minutes to fill out the form. Why is it taking him so long? So, I would occasionally go to his room and interrupt him playing video games and ask him about the status of his completion of the voter registration card. He would respond, "I am working on it, Mom."

Weeks passed and he still had not given me his completed voter registration form. I began to get frustrated, because of the seemingly endless delay. I went up to his room and with a firm tone, I said, "Why can't you stop playing those video games for a brief moment and complete your voter registration card?" He responded, "I am working on it, Mom." Well, that was not acceptable this time, and I knew that he knew that I was not pleased.

I was in the kitchen and my son approached and handed me his form. I said, "Thank you, finally!" I told him, "Don't you know how important it is to vote, especially considering the sacrifices made by people in the past?" Then, he responded, "Mom, this was a very difficult decision for me and I had to do a lot of research." I responded, "Research, why did you have to research to just register to vote?" Then he said, "Because I didn't know which political party I should join. I had to research the positions of the Republican and Democratic parties before I could complete the form." I said to him, "Why didn't you just do the same thing that I did and just register as an Independent?"

He looked at me right into my eyes and said words that would change my life over the next year. He said, "Mom, I don't want to be like you – I don't want to stand on the sideline of the political process, I want to make a choice, I want to stand for something. I decided that I would register as a Democrat, because I want to support the candidacy of Senator Obama. He is very intelligent and has good ideas for this country. Also, he is the only candidate who opposed the war from the start. He has a lot of good ideas. Maybe he would have a chance at winning the election if people like you would get off the sideline and help to get him elected. If you choose to do nothing, and they continue this war and maybe bring back the draft, how are you going to feel then if you didn't work to help stop this war? All your children are at the age to be drafted. Are you planning on staying on the sideline or working to help him bring about the change needed for my generation?"

I was not prepared for that response. Then he said, "Aren't you going to be a little lonely this year with all the children gone – you know the empty nest stuff. So, why don't you plan a party for Senator Obama, since you don't have the Valentine's Ball to do?"

I was stunned!

Soon after that exchange, I changed my voter registration from Independent to Democrat, so I could vote for Senator Obama in the primary, and I started to work for his election. I contacted the Obama office and requested authorization to host a special party (fundraiser) for him in April 2008. I contacted people locally and was directed to a person in the Washington, D.C. Obama campaign office who had the same name as my daughter, Courtney. She informed me that she did not have the authority to approve a public event past February 5th, the big Super Tuesday primary date, and that I would have to contact the main office in Chicago.

I contacted the person in the Chicago campaign office and spoke with a woman named Kim. I explained my request and she too said that they were not planning any event past the February Super Tuesday date. That was not acceptable, and I thought to myself, "These people don't understand that I have to do this event. I have to prepare Pennsylvania for Obama, because if they wait until after the Super Tuesday primary, it would be too late for me to lay the foundation to prepare them for the battle in this state. If he ended up needing this state to win the primary or general election, I had a lot of work to do before their people got here. I know where the lemons are buried and I know how to mobilize support to create many sweet jars of lemonade for him. But, I need to start now."

I sent her my information and event concept, and she finally agreed to allow me to do the April event.

I posted the event on the Obama website around January or February, and immediately started getting registrations, contributions, comments, and questions. I received several comments, phone calls and emails from people expressing their surprise at my planning an event in April when the February Super Tuesday would probably decide the election. Some people expressed shock that the campaign was so confident to believe that Obama would still be in the competition after the February Super Tuesday date.

I assured them that this event had nothing to do with the Obama campaign's desire to have an event scheduled in April or their over confidence in the potential election results. I told them that this had nothing to do with the campaign. This was something that I had to do, because of a conversation with my son. I told them, "But, you can be sure that if God called me into action, the battle was indeed going to occur here in Pennsylvania, and I am headed for the front lines to fight this war."

Those contacts turned into support.

I guess my bold request for that April event pleased someone in the Obama Chicago office, because shortly after my call to them, the first official Obama staffer arrived in Philadelphia and contacted me to let me know about a special meeting that was going to be held in a few days. At that meeting, I was told by the staff that I was going to be one of Obama's delegates to the Democratic National Convention in Denver. I was shocked. I worked hard to get petitions signed for Obama and for me, so we could both be on the Pennsylvania April 22, 2008 ballot.

We both had to get voters to elect us on the Pennsylvania Primary election day. I was elected as an Obama delegate, receiving the most votes of all other Obama delegates in Congressional District 7, including elected officials on the ballot. Obama won the county, but lost the state in the Primary. After talking to my son on the phone after the Pennsylvania Primary election, while he was still away in college in New York, he was disappointed about the loss. He once again challenged me and asked if I had done everything that I could do to get Obama elected. He just couldn't understand the loss. He was taking the loss personally.

Oh no, I can't let Obama lose Pennsylvania – especially not because of race. I didn't know if I could handle my children believing that they would be limited because of their race. I had done everything possible to raise them in a reconciled social, educational and religious environment. I didn't talk about reconciliation to them; I created a life for them that exemplified living a life of reconciliation – in the community, in school, and in church. I had done everything in my power to prepare them for a reconciled society, a post-civil rights society that I dreamed of for my children. I didn't want them to have any of my painful experiences.

I reevaluated my work for the campaign during the primary and concluded that my son was right again. I had not done my best. Yes – I had worked tirelessly with little or no sleep, but I had more to give. There was more that I could do. After the primary election, I expanded my work for the campaign state-wide, working in multiple capacities. I couldn't lose Pennsylvania again.

An unexpected pleasant moment occurred on the campaign trail that I will never forget. Michelle Obama was scheduled to appear at Haverford College which is located in the Philadelphia suburbs. The local campaign staff gave my husband and me VIP tickets to attend the event. We entered the building and found some great seats close to the stage. I had to get up to look for a friend to give her a ticket, so she could enter the event. As I walked toward the door where I had entered, I made eye contact with the tall, attractive white lady, and we walked toward each other. We stood there and she asked me if I was Gail Conner, Ms. Rena's friend. I said, "Yes." I was surprised by this stranger's statement. Then, she said that Ms. Rena was her prayer partner. I said that Ms. Rena was my prayer partner, too. We laughed over our mutual friend. Our prayer partner, Ms. Rena, a black Christian woman whom we were both talking about was my children's Sunday school teacher at my church in Pennsylvania. This lady lived in Chicago, Illinois and we both had the same prayer partner, Ms. Rena. You are a very special person if you have Ms. Rena as a prayer partner.

During that same event, another memorable thing happened. After Michelle Obama finished speaking, she was shaking hands near where we were seated. I am only 5'2" inches, so I could not get past the crowd, but my husband was able to get close enough to Mrs. Obama to give her a message. He told her that his wife told him that she was married to her husband, Senator Obama, until November 4th, 2008. To his surprise, Mrs. Obama responded, "Be patient with her." My husband was shocked at the response, and we both were delighted at her sense of humor.

I had forgotten that I had made that statement to my husband so many months before. But, if I was going to meet the challenge of my son, to do everything in my power to facilitate the election of Senator Obama, then some things had to be put on hold until the campaign was over. So, my best explanation to him of how much personal capital I was going to invest in this political process this year was that I was going to be married to Senator Obama. He knew what it meant to have my full commitment in marriage, so that let him know immediately that I was very serious and to stand back, because I was functioning like a political demolition woman, allowing nothing to stand in my way to achieve the desired results.

A Pennsylvania general election victory would be my birthday present to my son. His birthday was November 5th, the day after the general election in 2008. When he awakened on Wednesday morning, November 5th, I intended to have a victory for him, his generation and future generation. I wasn't the only one who considered the election of Obama his birthday present. Apparently, his sister sent him an electronic note, wishing him a happy birthday and indicated that his birthday gift was Senator Obama's victory. My son, Daniel, called me and wondered if he was going to get any other gifts, because Courtney had told him that his birthday gift was the election of

Senator Obama as President. I assured him that he would get something else from me, too.

I had faith in the American people that we were better than our bloodstained history. We were almost a reconciled, healed nation. I had to finish the job in my lifetime, so that my children's generation would only read about how things used to be in the history books, but would not have personal experiences that continued that painful legacy. I was drawing a line in the political sand of history, this year, this time in Pennsylvania and losing was not an option. I gave it my best. I gave it my all, and I finished the job before me. My journey in life had ended for me in 2008. I had taken my rightful place on the front line of change, not the sideline. I plowed the road, so that my son, who challenged me and my other children and their generation, could travel a less bumpy road. A road prepared by my generation for the next generation.

Happy Birthday, Daniel!

CHAPTER 11

The Unexpected Result of Slavery

H$_2$O

H$_2$O for scientists represents two molecules of hydrogen plus one molecule of oxygen, which results in the life-sustaining element (water) that is required for existence and without which there would be no plants, no animals, no you and no me.

However, there is another combination of H$_2$O that has divided nations, countries and people for centuries. This combination results in a lethal blow for those who have been identified to be a conquered people.

H$_2$O = 2 Part Holy, 1 Part Oppression

The two parts holy was good, but when combined with the one part oppression, the result was very bad for those targeted, creating a legacy of pain that engulfed both the oppressed and the oppressor.

The Doubled-Edged Sword — The Pulpit and Court!

What are the two most powerful systems in society? The pulpit and the court! One system controls your mind and the other controls your body. Both of these powerful systems worked in unison for centuries in the United States of America.

Judges are the most important leaders in this country, because they directly impact the lives of every person in this country, and their decisions determine whether I am **FREE** or **SLAVE**. The deafening silence from the pulpit or spoken words to support an unjust system emboldens the power of the court decisions. At least, that is the way that it was for hundreds of years.

Let's look back at our American history and the Dred Scott decision. In March of 1857, one hundred and one years before I was born, Chief Justice Roger B. Taney of the U.S. Supreme Court stated that blacks **COULD NEVER BE CITIZENS OF THE UNITED STATES**.

A summary of the DRED SCOTT decision is below:

In March of 1857, the United States Supreme Court, led by Chief Justice Roger B. Taney, declared that all blacks — slaves as well as free — were not and could never become citizens of the United States. The court also declared the 1820 Missouri Compromise unconstitutional, thus permitting slavery in all of the country's territories. The case before the court was that of Dred Scott v. Sanford. Dred Scott, a slave who had lived in the free state of Illinois and the free territory of Wisconsin before moving back to the slave state of Missouri, had appealed to the Supreme Court in hopes of being granted his freedom. Taney — a staunch supporter of slavery and intent on protecting southerners from northern aggression — wrote in the Court's majority opinion that, because Scott was black, he was not a citizen and therefore had no right to sue. The framers of the Constitution, he wrote, believed that blacks "had no rights, which the white man was bound to respect; and that the Negro might justly and lawfully be reduced to slavery for his benefit. He was bought and sold and treated as an ordinary article of merchandise and traffic, whenever profit could be made by it." Referring to the language in the Declaration of Independence that includes the phrase, "all men are created equal," Taney reasoned that "it is too clear for dispute, that the enslaved African race were not intended to

be included, and formed no part of the people who framed and adopted this declaration ..."
Abolitionists were incensed. Although disappointed, Frederick Douglass, found a bright side to the decision and announced, "my hopes were never brighter than now." For Douglass, the decision would bring slavery to the attention of the nation and was a step toward slavery's ultimate destruction.[19]

Justice Taney was a Christian (Catholic), but his views did not represent the views of all Christians, including Catholics.[20] This was most definitely a lemon for the slave Dred Scott and every person in slavery in this country, including my ancestors. But, God turned that bad decision made by man into lemonade for an enslaved race of people that included my ancestors. This judicial decision became the social spark that created a fire that burned down the system of slavery – the Civil War. It took the shedding of **blood** of thousands of people to undo the harm caused by the judicial decision of the U.S. Supreme Court, which was led by Justice Taney. It became lemonade for an entire race of people, including me, because this court decision resulted in the Civil War.

This was one of those national counterintuitive moments that engulfed a nation, leaving no place for anyone to hide from the truth of a national social injustice. I come from the ashes of that historic war. But for the Civil War, I would not be able to share this message of hope with you, because reading and writing was illegal for someone like me. It would take the combined effort of thousands of people over a hundred years, working together to correct past wrongs and free a people. The Dred Scott decision had a counterintuitive result – both negative and positive – something good coming from something bad. God used a bad court decision that initially divided the country, but ultimately united a country, creating a foundation that would make our nation a world leader generations later.

Another example of a counterintuitive result is Christ's crucifixion on the cross. Jesus was executed on the cross during ancient times that involved nailing the person to an upright cross and leaving him to die a slow, painful and agonizing death. You can either look at the death of Christ on the cross as victimization or as victory. If the story ended with his death on the cross, reflecting only upon the pain and suffering that was caused to someone who was innocent and had committed no crime, would focus on the victimization. However, if you believe that the story continued even after his death and that he rose again on the third day on Easter Sunday morning, then you would see the victory! I know for many, it may be difficult to comprehend this counterintuitive historical moment. But, for me, that moment in time is also my legacy.

I guess you are wondering how this can be my legacy, since I am a black woman of African descent. Jesus was Jewish and I am not Jewish. Well, if you focus on my race, you will miss the entire point. Jesus' death and resurrection is my legacy because...

He was innocent of any wrongdoing.
He was wrongfully accused.
He was oppressed.
He was despised.
He was rejected.
He suffered.
He was afflicted by being caused severe mental and physical distress.
He was lead like a lamb to the slaughter.
He was a man of sorrow.
He forgave those who caused him harm.
He saved me because of his death on the cross and resurrection!
He gave me a legacy of forgiveness and eternal life that I passed on to my children – a legacy that can't be taken away by the hand of man.

Maybe it would be appropriate to be reminded of how Christ suffered under the hands of rulers and maybe this will help you cope with your struggles in life.

Isaiah 53:1-10

1 Who has believed our message and to whom has the arm of the LORD been revealed?
2 He grew up before him like a tender shoot, and like a root out of dry ground. He had no beauty or majesty to attract us to him, nothing in his appearance that we should desire him.

3 He was despised and rejected by men, a man of sorrows, and familiar with suffering. Like one from whom men hide their faces he was despised, and we esteemed him not.
4 Surely he took up our infirmities and carried our sorrows, yet we considered him stricken by God, smitten by him, and afflicted.
5 But he was pierced for our transgressions, he was crushed for our iniquities; the punishment that brought us peace was upon him, and by his wounds we are healed.
6 We all, like sheep, have gone astray, each of us has turned to his own way; and the LORD has laid on him the iniquity of us all.
7 He was oppressed and afflicted, yet he did not open his mouth; he was led like a lamb to the slaughter, and as a sheep before her shearers is silent he did not open his mouth.
8 By oppression and judgment he was taken away. And who can speak of his descendants? For he was cut off from the land of the living; for the transgression of my people he was stricken.
9 He was assigned a grave with the wicked, and with the rich in his death, though he had done no violence, nor was any deceit in his mouth.
10 Yet it was the Lord's will to crush him and cause him to suffer, and though the LORD makes his life a guilt offering, he will see his offspring and prolong his days,

and the will of the LORD will prosper in his
hand.

Jesus was a man of sorrow and the African-slaves
and their descendants have been a people of sorrow.
Bearing the burden of the cross of oppression and
racism just for being born, just for existing, just for
breathing, just for being born with a tan, just for
having African **blood** in our veins.

The death and resurrection of Jesus provided
an opportunity for healing and reconciliation for
anyone who makes a personal decision to accept
Christ in his or her life. The journey of Christ on this
earth included the most derogative, severe, oppressive, hostile, evil treatment and pain imaginable –
including death on the cross by crucifixion. But, that
was not the end of the journey for Jesus. Yes, he was
oppressed, mistreated, wrongfully accused, beaten,
and murdered on the cross and hung between two
criminals. But, he rose again on Sunday morning,
resulting in salvation for us all. His death and resurrection through the shedding of his innocent **blood**
provided all people with the opportunity for salvation if we accept Christ as Lord and Savior.

Thus, something good came from something bad
– **Salvation!**

The same is true for the African-Negro slave.
The harsh, evil, oppressive, inhumane enslavement,
and treatment of a race of people for hundreds of
years, and subsequent hostility after slavery were
intended for bad. But, God turned the evil intentions
of man into good, by exposing our people to the

Scriptures, and salvation was made available even to us. We gained our freedom through Jesus Christ, while still enslaved and oppressed. We gained eternal life in heaven even though we had no life on earth. We gained love from God when there was no love for us on earth. We gained peace in the midst of the storm that seemed would never end. We gained hope for future generations and prayed that our children would have a better life to live. We gained unbelievable strength and courage to fight on, even when winning the battle seemed impossible.

The Unexpected Result of Slavery

Did any aspect of slavery create a counterintuitive result?

Was there an unexpected result for the descendants of the African slave?

Did God turn the very sour lemons of an entire race of people into lemonade?

My answer to that question is YES!

We who are descendants of slaves now live in the most powerful country and one of the wealthiest countries in the world – the United States!

The buying power of 39 million African-Americans is anticipated to hit $1.1 trillion by 2012. [21]

My ancestors' unfortunate capture resulted in their being sold into slavery, but now, generations later, I am benefiting from being in this land at this time in history.

With our presence in this land, we can cross the waters, this time willingly, to help those in need. With the global marketplace directly impacting the lives of people thousands of miles away, we can use our gifts and talents to tend to the wounds of those in need – as missionaries, businesswomen, businessmen, scientists, engineers, social workers, lawyers, doctors, researchers, environmentalists, and architects...

The resources on the Continent of Africa have always been of interest to other nations. We must play a role in the future of the African Continent, so that their resources benefit, instead of harm, the people of the land. We must make the commitment and find the way to turn from being orphans belonging to no one to adopted daughters and sons whom anyone would be proud to embrace and call their own.

I know that we have a legacy of slavery that we wish never existed, and that carrying the burden of that legacy comes with a heavy price: broken spirit, broken dreams, and broken you. There is an alternative. Give that burden to God right now. Just leave all that pain and hurt at the altar, and let him deal with the hard hearts of men and women.

God dealt with the hard heart of Pharaoh in Exodus, when he would not release his people from bondage. Pharaoh refused to let his people go, and the land of Egypt was hit with plagues, until the one in leadership got God's message. If you truly trust God, then let it go.

The Bible was intended to be an instrument of control of the oppressed slaves. Instead, the Bible yielded an unintended result. It gave the slave and those of us who are descendants of slaves, who have accepted Jesus as our Lord and Savior – **FREEDOM** and **SALVATION!** And, the bonus gift is being a citizen of the 21st Century United States of America. Wow! What a blessing!

CHAPTER 12

HEALING PARTIES

Ever since my daughter's first birthday, I would throw a party. Not just any party, but a party that would express my love in such a way that when I was no longer on this earth, she would know that I loved her from the moment she was conceived in my womb. As my family expanded to three children, the birthday party tradition continued. I wanted to celebrate life not death. I never understood why people would spend so much money on a funeral, while at the same time, they would never bother to express that same level of love at the same expense for the same person, while they are still alive – what a tragedy.

It is no secret among my friends that I hate funerals! I hate everything about the process: the flowers for the person (who can't smell them), the beautiful words of affection and love (for someone who can't hear them), the elaborate expense of the burial (for someone who can't see it), having people look over your body, and sometimes take photos that later end up on the Internet (that you may not even consider a friend). It is the most vulnerable state of existence, the last days of your physical body being on earth in the flesh in this lifetime, as we know it. It is an irrational process.

Of course, there are those who would say that the funeral is for the family, not for the person being grieved. Well, if that is the case, why have the flowers adorning the casket? Why not send the flowers to the family members that are grieving? I believe that it is just a tradition that people practice without giving any thought to whether the tradition is beneficial or harmful. But, many people are not flexible enough to consider changing the long-time tradition.

Do you want your children to really be exposed to this horrible day in their life? Do you really want your children to be shackled with a tradition that they may not want to go through either? Do you really want their last memory of you to be the sight of a lifeless body, lying in front of a pulpit, adorned with flowers that you can't smell or see?

For me, the answer is an emphatic NO! For me, a funeral would be the worst possible way you could show your love for me. In fact, having a traditional funeral, for me, would mean that you never understood my values or understood me.

I value life NOT death. If you value life, why don't you begin to act like it – TODAY! Stop rushing through each day and failing to experience all that God has created for your pleasure. This day will never return. You can't press the rewind button and capture a lost moment in time. Stop spending so much time in front of the TV, at work or with people you don't even know, and spend time doing the things that make you happy and give you joy.

Spend time creating moments of joy for others that will create wonderful memories for them. This is worth more than all the gold, silver and riches on earth. This is what I decided to start doing years ago, initially by accident and intentionally thereafter.

As I said, I had always thrown my daughter a birthday party each year. These were no ordinary birthday parties. I would spend a year planning them. I started doing these parties beginning on her first birthday. She couldn't possibly understand the joy I had when I finally found out I was pregnant for the first time. I married when I was a junior in college. When I finished my degree I was ready to have children, but it didn't happen right away.

My best friend, Spring knew that I loved animals – especially dogs. She also knew that my husband, Curtis, did not care for animals – especially those that live inside the house. So, only my best friend, Spring, would have the nerve to do what only she could do for me. She got the puppy from the Farmer's Market and arrived at my doorstep with a little bundle of joy in her arms as a gift for me. It was a puppy and she told Curtis, "You had better not say a word, because this gift is for Gail. She needs this puppy." Of course, Curtis didn't say a word and my gift was the best thing that a friend could do for me at that time in my life. The puppy was a German Shepherd and Husky mix. She was beautiful! I named my puppy Buffy.

Men will never understand the bond between girlfriends. It is like having a soul mate that you can share girl things with and never feel threatened. If you are blessed to have a girlfriend with whom you can pray, share and just do fun things and laugh, then you are truly blessed. This type of friend is as rare as a black pearl. She can help you stay out of despair when dealing with burdens and obstacles in life.

So, guess what? I got my puppy, Buffy, I got pregnant! When all hope is gone and you stop struggling to find the answers through man – God steps in and answers your prayer. That is how I got my little daughter, Courtney, so I wanted to celebrate this gift of life at every opportunity. My way of celebrating was with the annual grand birthday party.

My family expanded, because I couldn't stop getting pregnant. It seemed that I was pregnant every 18 months. I had two sons, Brian and then Daniel. I carried a diaper bag for six years. I did all the traditional stuff, because I wanted to experience the joy of motherhood in every possible way. With the natural childbirth, breast feeding, the Lamaze classes, and the focal point during labor (which doesn't work, because there is no focal point that is strong enough to overcome the feeling of pain which is like pulling your lip over your head without any pain killers), my strength weakened significantly through the process and by our third child, I decided to take a "rain check" on the natural stuff. The spirit was willing, but the body abandoned the cause.

OK – be careful what you ask for when you pray. I had wanted a child so badly. I told God that if he just blessed me with a child, I would have as many as he would allow me to have. He answered and it seems that I was becoming a baby machine. My Grandmother Viola told my husband that two children were enough (I guess that was a lot of children since she only had one child – my dad). I was considered the Brady Bunch in our family when I had our third child. But, all three children were beautiful gifts from God, so I expressed my love every year through the birthday party events for each of them.

Courtney decided when she was in the fourth grade that she didn't want anymore birthday parties.

What – no more parties? What do you mean no more parties? Then, she said to me. "Mom, your parties are traumatizing, because I never know what is going to jump out or what type of 'special surprise' you are going to have. So, I don't want any more birthday parties." I agreed to her request, even though it made me a little sad. I still have the boys' birthday parties to do, so that will be fine, I guess.

My children were attending a Quaker School at that time. I planned several social events over a couple of years, including two Annual Giving Balls (The Mardi Gras Cruise Ball in 1996 and the Roaring 20s Ball in 1997). I also planned a Teachers Appreciation Luncheon, and surprised them with an "Elvis Presley" look-alike as special entertainment.

But, none of those events replaced the void that was left from not being able to entertain my daughter. Courtney was entering middle school and she was not attending any social events – I couldn't do the birthday party and there were no school dances. So, I asked the Head of School, a wonderful woman, Ginny who truly loved children, if I could plan a Valentine's Dance for the middle school students. She told me that a dance would be wonderful, but they didn't have such an event included in their school budget. I told her that my husband and I would sponsor the dance if she would allow us to make that gift to the school. She agreed without hesitation.

So, I began my preparation process. I was so excited. Since my daughter wouldn't let me entertain her with a birthday party, I would entertain the entire middle school, and indirectly get to entertain her anyway. Maybe this would work. She wouldn't be the focal point of the event. She never liked being the center of attention. She is very frugal anyway and will probably end up living in some foreign country, doing missionary work someday, so my parties just didn't match her personality. I would later learn that even though my daughter didn't care for my elaborate events, both of our boys, their classmates and friends would come to love them, and it would eventually turn into a tradition for them.

The school gym would be the place for this first Valentine's Ball. Oh my, how do I transform this boring gym into something exciting and fun for the teens? I went to work, did my research, and picked the first Valentine's Ball theme – *The Love Boat*.

I hired a decorator and a DJ, and I found special entertainment (something to traumatize the teens later during the evening, so they would learn to never leave one of my events early). I also hired a photographer (you've got to have pictures if you want to create memories). Of course I had to get them food that they would love. It was all so exciting. The only thing left was the event. Would the teens show up? It was a success!

The teens loved it, especially the themed decorations and the surprise entertainment. They loved being entertained and I loved entertaining them. The teens loved it so much, and I think my daughter Courtney did, too, even though she would never admit it. One of the teen's families was moving to another state out west. The daughter was a good friend of my daughter and her classmate. One of the conditions of the relocation that the daughter made with her parents was that she would be able to fly back to Pennsylvania to attend the Valentine's Ball. When the Valentine's Ball was special enough to this student to make such a request, I knew that I was fulfilling a special need for those teenagers.

I also noticed something else. I was enjoying the preparation and planning for the parties so much that I began to need to do the parties as much as the teens enjoyed having them. It was therapeutic for me. It was a distraction from my struggles in life. I was entertaining white teens, black teens, middle class teens, wealthy teens, poor teens, Christian teens, Jewish teens, and teens without any religious affiliation. There was nothing to hinder our being together, just to enjoy this special moment in time, created just for them.

I continued to do the Valentine's Balls every year. The only conditions to be able to attend the party were that the teens had to:

Look Nice,
Be Nice, and
Act Nice

And I would give them a party to die for!

There was a special element that I wanted to add to the events, but the teens lacked the social skills to participate in what I wanted to do. My daughter moved on to high school. Unlike my daughter, my oldest son Brian, and his classmates had heard about the dances in elementary school and had come to look forward to the day when the dances would be for them. So, they waited with anticipation to attend the Valentine's Balls once they were in middle school.

That is why this next level of entertainment would be appropriate for this group of teenagers. I could increase the complexity of the events. They had potential, but I needed to prepare them before the event. So, I asked the Head of School if I could bring professional dancers into the school and use class time to teach the middle school students how to do swing dancing? I couldn't believe it when she agreed. What an adventure!

These wallflowers, who didn't know how to interact in social settings as males and females, turned into dancing machines. It was awesome. At first, they were afraid to touch their dance partner, and then they transformed into these teens that I didn't know existed. The dances emerged into a new level, and I was able to do even more elaborate events with this group.

As my youngest son and his classmates were attending elementary school, waiting on their chance to enter middle school and have their special Valentine's Balls, something changed. As a family, we decided that he would not be attending the same middle school that his brother and sister attended. He would be attending a different school, so that the transition from middle school to high school would be easier for him than it had been for his sister, because curriculums between schools were so different.

Daniel visited other schools and decided that he would like to attend the same school that his older sister was attending, with one condition. His statement puzzled us. What could possibly be a condition that our youngest son would want that would determine whether he would go willingly to another school? We were shocked to discover the condition: to continue having the Valentine's Balls, so that he and his classmates could have the same experience that Courtney, Brian and their classmates had. He said that it would not be fair to deny him and his classmates the Valentine's Balls after they had waited for the day when they would be the focus of the events. We agreed to this condition and that is how the Valentine's Balls became an annual tradition for so many teens over the past 12 years. An event starting out entertaining about 50 teenagers grew into an annual event, entertaining as many as 150 teens.

I have literally never really had to chaperone them. Their attire and behavior improved with each year, until they started offering to help me during the events and giving me hugs and warm words of thanks before, during and after the events. The cards, emails, smiles, and their playing along with me each year has been a wonderful experience.

You see, they didn't just get a special invitation each year to invite them to the Valentine's Ball. They received an invitation embedded with clues, so they would have to send me their guess of the party theme. They wouldn't know if they were correct until they arrived at the Valentine's Ball. If they were correct, or just gave me a good analysis, I would have a special gift for the winners. But, I would give the gift privately, because I never wanted anyone who didn't get the answer to feel like they were losers. The purpose was to get everyone involved and to create a memorable experience. They knew that I always had some type of theme party favors for them anyway, and my traditional Valentine's candy treats. So, no one left the event without the opportunity to receive special treats and a gift.

Those parties provided me with emotional healing and gave me an opportunity to watch teens from different races, religions and economic backgrounds, interact socially at parties together, without the cares of the world on their shoulders. They didn't know what was waiting for them in the harsh world and I wanted to delay that experience as long as possible, and while they are waiting to grow up, to create some memories that they could reflect on that no one could take away from them.

Maybe one day, when these teenagers become adults, they will remember the Valentine's Balls that that black woman gave for them and maybe create positive memories and relationships to provide reconciliation and healing, if needed, in their generation. Maybe some of the memories that I have had an opportunity to create for them will replace some of the bad memories in their lives. It doesn't matter if the teen is rich or poor, the race, religion or gender, the needs are all the same – the need for extraordinary love.

These are the types of moments that I dreamed about sharing with my white counterparts when I was growing up. But, I wasn't invited to the parties of my white classmates. When the invitations were passed out in class or they would whisper about them to each other, I would dream of being invited, of being included. Dreams that would never be, because of the racially hostile time period I was born in. But, God gave me a new gift – the gift of event planning in a way that only I can do, because, like the beauty of the lands in Africa, I appreciate special memories and value time in a way that others may fail to appreciate.

So, with each event, the teens experienced a little portion of love that I had to share with others that I couldn't share as a child during desegregation. I lost those times as a child in the segregated era that I lived in. But, I got to create special moments and re-live them as an adult through these teens. They will never know how much I gained each time I saw them smile or each time they dressed up so nicely, because they knew that I would notice how much effort they had made to please me by their lady-like and gentlemanly appearance. They knew that they had to behave at a level that I expected, because to require me to discipline them would break my heart and take away my joy.

Discipline was never really required. They knew that they could feel comfortable dancing, eating, sharing, and laughing at my events, because they knew that I spent all this time to create this special moment in time – just for them. They knew that they would be treated as kings and queens for at least one special night each year. Somehow, I would manage to make it happen.

The events started in a school gym and moved to various venues around the area with sometimes the venues even being one of the clues to the party theme.

The Valentine's Balls were always held in February and always on a Friday night.

I wonder if the teens got my final clue. Why did I always do the event in February? Why did I choose Valentine to celebrate, instead of some other date? I wonder if they got the final clue.

The party was always in February, because it was Black History Month and I wanted to create a positive memory for them to displace the potentially negative images that they may be exposed to in their lives. I also chose February, because that is the month where love is expressed and teenagers need a lot of love in their lives, especially during this period of time when they may struggle between two worlds – childhood and adulthood.

This was my way of facilitating reconciliation. I used my parties to heal damaged spirits, broken hearts, and bad memories. It was my way of healing old wounds that I had. I gave to them, but in return, I received more than they will ever know.

Here are a few Valentine's Ball Themes that I created for the teens over 12 years:

A FEW SHARED – VALENTINE'S BALL THEMES

Camelot

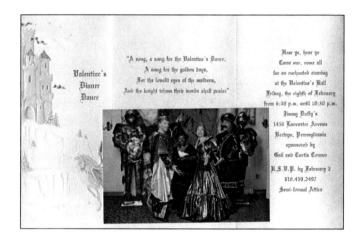

Alice in Wonderland

Winter Wonderland

YOU ARE CORDIALLY INVITED TO THE

Blue Jeans & Diamonds

VALENTINE'S DINNER DANCE

FRIDAY, FEBRUARY 7, 2003
6:30 P.M. UNTIL 11:00 P.M.

JIMMY DUFFY'S & SON'S INC.
1456 LANCASTER AVENUE
BERWYN, PA 19312

What Am I?

GLASS POOL, ICY THROUGH
BLANKETS OF WHITE
FROZEN DEW
TINKLING ICE
IT SEEMS LIKE PARADISE WITH
SPARKLING DIAMONDS ALL AROUND

THE EXCITEMENT IN OUR HEARTS DID GROW
WHEN WE DREAMED OF THE TIME WE WILL SHARE WITH
TEENAGE FRIENDS
DRESSED IN OUR FINEST · BLUE JEANS AND DIAMONDS

LILI'UOKALANI - The Last Hawaiian Queen

On the Sandwich Isles the last dynasty fell
As I tried to preserve paradise's culture that prevailed
Come celebrate an evening of royal delight
Because I am one of a kind -- indeed I am a royal capitol delight

2004 Valentine's Dinner Dance

Friday, February 6, 2004
6:30 p.m. until 11:00 p.m.

J&J Catering
880 Springdale Drive
Exton, Pennsylvania 19431

Sponsored by
Gail & Curtis Conner
610-459-2497

RSVP on or before Friday, January 23, 2004   semi-formal attire

Email your "guess" of the 2004 Valentine's Dinner Dance theme to:
gmcgcenvi@aol.com

St. Valentine

THEME: ST. VALENTINE
...wrote a letter from prison to a young girl that he fell in love with in Ancient Rome 269 A.D. and signed the letter "FROM YOUR VALENTINE"

THE EMPEROR EXTENDS A WARM INVITATION FOR YOU TO ATTEND A SPECIAL EVENING CELEBRATION

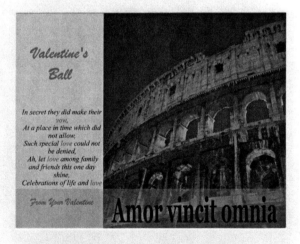

Valentine's Ball

In secret they did make their vow,
At a place in time which did not allow,
Such special love could not be denied,
Ah, let love among family and friends this one day shine,
Celebrations of life and love

From Your Valentine

Amor vincit omnia

LOVE CONQUERS EVERYTHING!

Roaring 50s

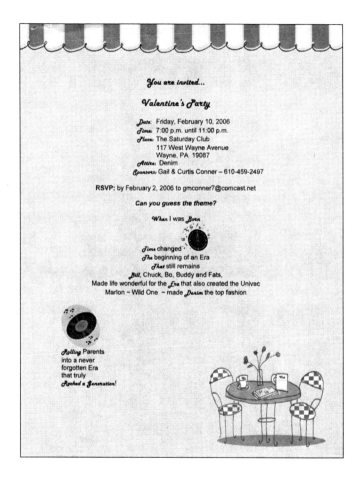

You are invited...

Valentine's Party

Date: Friday, February 10, 2006
Time: 7:00 p.m. until 11:00 p.m.
Place: The Saturday Club
117 West Wayne Avenue
Wayne, PA 19087
Attire: Denim
Sponsors: Gail & Curtis Conner – 610-459-2497

RSVP: by February 2, 2006 to gmconner7@comcast.net

Can you guess the theme?

When I was *Born*

Time changed
The beginning of an Era
That still remains
Bill, Chuck, Bo, Buddy and Fats,
Made life wonderful for the *Era* that also created the Univac
Marlon ~ Wild One ~ made *Denim* the top fashion

Rolling Parents
into a never
forgotten Era
that truly
Rocked a Generation!

I wrote a special poem that I included on "The Last Dance" Valentine's invitation. The Last Valentine's Ball didn't have a theme. It was a party filled with memories and reflection.

POEM: *THE LAST DANCE*

(As special poem written for special teens who hold a special place in my heart)

The Time has come to say good-bye.
We must be strong – We must not cry.
The years have passed – how quickly they passed.
Oh, the years of wonderful memories that I thought would last and last.
As you travel to your next stage in life.
Take with you the memories of the Sweet Last Valentine's Dance!
May you never forget the joy, the laughter, the dancing, each other…

A FEW SPECIAL NOTES

Dear Mr. and Mrs. Conner,

Thank you so much for the Valentine Party you threw for us! I have always had a wonderful time at them! Since my time at Woodlynde I have appriciated everything you have done for us! I don't know what I'll do for the next few years! I'll miss all of you! It's been a joy having Brian as a classmate and friend and I wish him the best for his future! Thank you again, and for all you've done!

Love,

Lindsay Adams

Lindsay Elizabeth Adams

Dear Mr. and Mrs. Conner,
Thank you so much for having me every year to your Valentine Dance. It's always a joy to be there! Can't wait to be in the fashoin show! It's going to be so much fun!
Love, Lindsay Adams

P.S. - Mrs. Connor, I'm extreemly sorry about cutting the Pineapple. I hope you will accept my apology.

Thank You

Dear Mr. and Mrs. Conner, Brian and Don;

Thank you very much for inviting me to your Valentines party. Everyone had a great time and it was nice seeing everyone from Woodlynde again.

I really appreciate you putting together the party every year, I always look forward to it. The food was delicous and the Super's Dance Team was awesome.

Thanks again.
David [illegible]

Dear Conner family,

I wanted to thank you for throwing such a great party. I had a lot of fun and I know all of my friends did as well. It was thoughtful of you as well as extremely generous.

Thanks again,

Annie Berardi

Annie Berardi

February 26, 07

Dear Gail, Curtis and Danny

Rye Biddle your beloved grandson, came home from your beautiful party raving about it — Imagine 12 years of parties each carefully thought out for your guests pleasure and enrichment. The food — sit down — lovely decoration and all friends together — what more could you ask. Bless you and Thank you

Barbara Rye & family

Victoria Mary Udvarhelyi

Dear Mr. and Mrs. Conner,

Thank you for another amazing Valentine's Dance!! From the music to the food, everything was so nice, and I had a great time! Its so nice of you to have a party like this (we all look forward to it every year!!) Anyways, thanks again, and i hope to see you some time soon.

Sincerely,
Tony Udvarhelyi

213

CHAPTER 13

REFLECTION

Our family was sitting around the table having dinner, watching television, and talking about the school year. The telephone rang, I answered the call and said, "Hello." The person on the other end of the call identified herself as Mrs. Terry. I whispered to my husband, "It's Mrs. Terry, a guidance counselor from our high school on the telephone." She asked how Curtis and I were doing, and I told her that we were fine. Then, she said that she had to give us a call and let us know how proud she was of both Curtis and me. She said that she had seen my picture on the cover of *Black Enterprise Magazine* (August 1998), read the article, and had to find us and tell us that she was extremely proud of our accomplishments.

This was such a wonderful call from an extraordinary woman who had guided my husband and me during those high school years when it was time to move into adulthood and attend college. I knew that she had directed me, but after the call, my husband and I talked about how Mrs. Terry impacted our lives. He shared with me that she had also directed him to attend Stillman College in Tuscaloosa (the only historically black Presbyterian college in the United States) which was the perfect place for him to study biology and participate in the music program that allowed him to travel across the United States, singing with the college choir. He even sang at a church in Pennsylvania that is not far from where we live today. He also pledged in the fraternity of Alpha Phi Alpha at Stillman College.

I realized that God had placed so many special people in my life over the years (my angels) that guided me along life's journey. I was not alone. God was watching and he also had others watching and caring for me along the way.

I wondered why I suffered so much for so long. Why there had been so many lemons in my short life? But, the suffering (lemons) made it possible for me to experience that special moment in time that no one else other than me could experience during my visit to Africa in 2006. It was a special gift, a precious gift that engulfed me with great joy.

The lemons that I encountered along my journey didn't matter anymore. I had been given everything that was really important in life: Christ the Savior for the redemption of my sins, parents and grandparents who loved me, in-laws who loved me, a wonderfully and loving extended family, a husband whom I prayed for and who could sing sweet melodies to me, three beautiful children who love the Lord, and even wonderful pets throughout my life to make me laugh and be happy when I didn't think happiness was available to someone like me.

Trusting God as my Savior so many years before was the best decision of my life. It was my rock and my foundation.

I just could not have made it through all the lemons in my life if I didn't believe in Jesus.

That decision saved my life!

I know that it is not politically correct to say the name of Jesus these days. But, I really don't care about what is politically correct. If anyone should have failed in life, considering the odds against me, it should have been me. But, here I stand before you.

I have been broken, but not destroyed. I have lost battles, but not the war. My hopes have been shattered by the hands of others, but God did not let me fail.

If that is not a miracle, as miraculous as the first miracle when Jesus turned water to wine, then you must be blind!

Surviving my life of lemons is a miracle!

I Am Not Alone

Job: The one who was persecuted, afflicted and endured adversity, who refused to deny the truth of God or reject God because of his circumstances.

Exodus: The suffering of a race of people who endured slavery and oppression with a leader who was insecure in his own abilities (especially his ability to speak). But, he put aside his weaknesses and gave up his comfortable life for the benefit of his people. He decided that freedom of a race of people was more important than his personal status or comfort. Moses is a person whom I admire the most, because he didn't give the people a talk or a map and tell them how to find their way to freedom. No, he allowed his life to be interrupted and he changed his destination and became a spokesperson for a race of people, by going before the powerful ruler of the land and demanding freedom for his people. He didn't give his people a map or a pep talk. Instead, he led the way.

Numbers: A reminder that freedom doesn't mean that you are out of the wilderness. No, freedom is just the first step toward healing of a race of people who have been in bondage. The people will have to endure great hardship to overcome the past and start a new life, with many being fearful of the unknown future and wanting to go back to the bondage of slavery, because that was all they knew. Sometimes, the trials and tribulations that come with freedom don't lead to the dreams that had danced in our heads. Those who are freed don't get to experience the benefit of their newfound freedom, because those who are in control are not quite ready to let go of the past. No, the newly freed person will only be able to start building a foundation for the benefit of future generations. We are working so that our children may see the Promised Land that we could only dream about. Our life is behind us. We can only hope for a better future for our children.

Psalms: Finding comfort and peace in praising God. We can find joy in God's gift of song and through worship. Our generation has the opportunity to bring forth joy in our land.

JOY ~ *Join to Overcome Yesterday*

Proverbs: Wisdom that is required for any foundation that is built on the solid rock of God.

Lamentations: Expressions of sadness and the misfortune of God's people.

Ezekiel: Encouragement that God will give us strength.

Daniel: The judgment of God.

Joel: Encouragement that God fulfills every desire.

Habakkuk:	When you struggle against adversity while embracing God.
John:	God is merciful and compassionate.
Peter:	A strong, firm rock, one who is established in God and is steadfast in God's truth.
Song of Songs:	We were not excluded from God's plan for salvation. Solomon's favorite wife was dark skinned and beautiful.

Beloved
How right they are to adore you!
Dark am I, yet lovely,
O daughters of Jerusalem,
Dark like the tens of Kedar,
Like the tent curtains of
Solomon.
Do not stare at me because I
Am dark, because I am darkened
By the sun.

I hope that those many parties that I gave to entertain hundreds of teenagers over the years will have a positive result on their lives and future relationships with others who may look a little different from them. I hope that those moments of pleasure provided a broader education of social inclusion and acceptance. The joy that I gave to others, the very best that I had to offer, is what I hope those teens, who are now adults, will take with them. God gave me his best, his only son to die on the cross for forgiveness of my sins. So, I give God my best. As I have told others – I only have two positions, on or off, because I don't drip!

Revelations 3:16

So, because you are lukewarm —
neither hot nor cold —

I am about to spit you out of my mouth.
I am not lukewarm.
When I am committed to something I give it my best, even when throwing a party for teenagers.

CHAPTER 14

A Husband's Viewpoint

How a Husband Sees His Wife – *A Virtuous Woman*

My wife is an incredible woman, who is also my partner in business. She started the business after learning that our third child would be coming. Gail had always wanted to start her own business and started an environmental firm in 1988. In 1995, she invited me to join her in the business. After this, she started law school and added that dimension to the business. Gail grew up in rural Alabama. She not only runs a business that was named JCPenney minority business supplier of the year, but she has chaired fundraising events at our kids' school, and does a Valentine's Dance every year that brings suburban and city kids together, to bridge not only the geographical and economic boundaries, but also racial. The Governor of Pennsylvania nominated

Gail to a volunteer citizens committee that oversees the Department of Environmental Protection policies for the state. She is a busy and strong woman who is also a proud mother of three and performs all her tasks exceptionally.

A wife of noble character
Who can find?
She is worth far more than rubies.
Her husband has full confidence in her
And lacks nothing of value,
She brings him good, not harm
All the days of her life.
Proverbs 31: 10-12

Written by Curtis R. Conner, March 2006

THE CLUES?

I confess – I am a dreamer, as an adult.
Dreamers are willing to take big risks for the possibility of achieving great gains. Because I am a dreamer, I am an "out-of-the-box" thinker who will aggressively create new approaches to solve problems or overcome obstacles that others may consider hopeless. I have learned the benefit of being a dreamer (*not only having hope, but also willing to do something to make that hope become a reality*). I like to provoke the dreams in others – children, teens and adults. But, many people are afraid to dream, afraid of disappointment, and afraid of failure. They only focus on what can't be done, instead of focusing on the possibilities. Of course, a dreamer can fail, but the possibility of success is far greater if your dreams encompass those God-given gifts and talents that make you special.

One way that I try to create a spark in those who are afraid to dream or who are too much of a realist to even consider the possibility of dreaming or imagining something that they can't see, smell and touch today, is by helping a person to re-visit those fond childhood memories when they laughed and played games without thinking about the cares of the world being on their shoulders. I have created nuggets (clues) in this manuscript that I hope will help you to renew the dreams within you.

Did you get the clue or clues embedded in this book? For those who know me and know about my Valentine's Balls and other events that I plan know that I always create an event that has a "theme" and I always, yes always, embed at least one clue in the event theme. I am not a woman of mystery, I am very predictable. But, I do not create anything without trying to provoke the participant to join me in my world by looking at things from a different perspective. So, my clues are intended to invite the participant to join me on my journey at a different level, by looking for the obvious message that you may read on an invitation that I create or this book that I wrote. I invite the reader to look for the other message that mere words can't share that is embedded in my message – The theme!

The clue is in the title of this book – **The theme**, just like my embedded message, would be in the title of the events that I have planned over the years, primarily for teenagers and sometimes for adults.

> <u>*The Clues*</u> –   *Why did I choose to use the colors and symbols on the cover?*
> *Why did I choose the title Healing Parties?*

The Answer – The same rules apply to you, the reader that have applied to all the teens and adults whom I have entertained over the years. You can only get the answer if you still know how to play. In order to know the answer, you have to guess.

So, email your guess to me at **HealingParties@ GailMConner.com** and if you make a "Good Faith" effort to figure out the answer using the clues, then I will email you the answer on the condition that you don't share the answer with others.

THE PINEAPPLE IS SIMILAR TO MANY
DREAMERS.
THERE MAY BE THE APPEARANCE OF
ROUGHNESS ON THE OUTSIDE,
BUT IF PROPERLY CULTIVATED AND NURTURED,
THE INSIDE DEVELOPS INTO AN "EXCELLENT
FRUIT."

Counterintuitive!

If I had to use one word to describe my life, my history, and my success, that word would be counter-intuitive. Counterintuitive means – *not in accordance with what would naturally be assumed or expected. It is when a result defies the traditional basic logic – it is something that is contrary to what common sense would suggest.*

ENDNOTES

[1] http://www.merriam-webster.
com/dictionary/counterintuitive

[2] http://www.southalabama.edu/archives/html/
manuscript/npvlguide.htm

[3] http://caselaw.lp.findlaw.com/scripts/getcase.
pl?court=US&vol=163&invol=537

[4] http://caselaw.lp.findlaw.com/scripts/getcase.
pl?court=us&vol=347&invol=483

[5] Book of Daniel Chapter 3, verses 19 – 30, New
International Version of the

Holy Bible, 1973, 1978, 1984, International Bible
Society.

[6] http://www.mobileazaleatrail.com/documents/
history.html

[7] http://www.pbs.org/wgbh/amex/missamerica/
peopleevents/e_mind.html

[8] Ibid

[9] http://www.johnstrange.com/edm310summer07/
hinds/history.html

[10] http://www.talladega.edu/index/cms-filesystem-
action/sacs/lib_fac.pdf

[11] Ibid

[12] http://www.talladega.edu/index/history

[13] http://www.jewishsf.com/content/2-0- /module/
displaystory/story_id/15372/edition_id/299/format/
html/displaystory.html

[14] http://www.pbs.org/itvs/fromswastikatojimcrow/
story.html

[15] http://www.sbc.net/resolutions/amResolution.
asp?ID=899

[16] http://www.wicn.
org/song-week/you-are-my-sunshine-1937

[17] http://www.news-medical.net/?id=34041

[18] http://www.reuters.
com/article/latestCrisis/idUSL23240037

[19] http://www.pbs.org/wgbh/aia/part4/4h2933.html

[20] http://www.freerepublic.
com/focus/f-religion/1881068/posts

[21] http://www.packagedfacts.
com/African-American-1475194/

Printed in the United States
217533BV00001B/1/P